twentysomething girl

Books by Donna Margaret Greene
from New Hope Publishers

Growing Godly Women

Letters from Campus

twentysomething girl

real advice on relationships,
careers, and life on your own

by

Donna Margaret Greene

new
hope
PUBLISHERS

Birmingham, Alabama

New Hope® Publishers
P. O. Box 12065
Birmingham, AL 35202-2065
www.newhopepublishers.com

Library of Congress Cataloging-in-Publication Data

ISBN: 1-56309-910-1

N054111 · 0105 · 7.5M1

Dedication

To all the twentysomethings

of the 21st century.

May you live life to the fullest,

shine as bright stars in the present,

and make the world a better place

for those yet to come.

contents

acknowledgments ∽ 9

introduction: Quarter-Life Crisis ∽ 13

chapter 1: Transition from College to the "Real World" ∽ 19

chapter 2: The Real World Is Looking for REAL People ∽ 25

chapter 3: Finding Contentment ∽ 31

chapter 4: Making the Most of Being Single ∽ 39

chapter 5: Dating Relationships ∽ 45

chapter 6: Marriage and Sex ∽ 55

chapter 7: Friendships ∽ 67

chapter 8: Trusting God with Your Life ∽ 77

chapter 9:   Relationship with God ～ 87

chapter 10:   Mistakes and Redemption ～ 97

chapter 11:   Seeking God's Plan for Your Life ～ 107

chapter 12:   Getting Involved ～ 115

chapter 13:   The Ins and Outs of Jobs ～ 121

chapter 14:   Finances ～ 133

chapter 15:   Careers and Ministry ～ 141

chapter 16:   Dealing with Loneliness ～ 149

chapter 17:   Quarter-Life Crisis Declared
             Over ～ 161

Contributors to This Book ～ 169

_acknowledgments

The writing of this book has been a true adventure. In a way, I have felt as if I were going "back to the future" as I have seen and experienced the lives of twentysomething girls in the early 21st century. As I wrote, I could not help but think of my own life as a twentysomething, living in New York City while flying for American Airlines as a stewardess. I watched in awe as the World Trade Towers were built over the years. The young women of today saw them fall within minutes. I was deeply concerned about Vietnam. Today, it is Iraq. I went to concerts in Central Park to hear bands that are the classics of today. Had I saved my clothes from that era of my life, I could wear them today and fit right in with the styles now. The world has changed, but the world is the same. One thing is certain: life is not a dress rehearsal. It is not a do-over. Once is all we get. But, if we live that life, really live it—one time is enough! Don't waste your life; invest it. Make the most of every moment and live it in light of eternity. Life in you twenties is a gift—a very special gift.

Although I did live a life of amazing opportunities and experiences and was exposed to a great deal of the world while flying and traveling while in my twenties, I could never have written this book without the help of the young women who are experiencing that phase of their lives right now. These are the ones who made this book possible.

Thank you to all of the young women who contributed to this book. You are literally spread across the United States from east to west and your writings came from Europe, Asia, South America, and Africa. Many of you I know personally, but so many were willing to open their hearts and share with a perfect stranger their deepest thoughts and heartfelt stories. Thank you. What a gift you have given in your vulnerability. I look forward to meeting you one day.

Thank you to the group of Birmingham girls who asked that this book be written and who helped to launch the campaign of getting advice from such a varied and diverse group of young women. Email really does work when it comes to spreading the news. Thank you for your persistence and ability to follow through with such a monumental task.

Thank you to the graduates of Washington and Lee University. I was privileged to visit your college campus for so many years as a guest speaker and to watch you evolve as individuals and in your walk with the Lord. You are in the "real world" now and I am still being blessed by your friendships and encouraged as I see you being "lights" for Christ wherever you are. Thank you for all that you contributed to this book in writing and for all that I gleaned from your lives. I look forward to our reunions for the rest of our lives.

Thank you to all of the "big city" girls who helped me to experience life as it is now for twentysomethings. What a treat to be allowed into your culture, which, I learned, was not for the faint hearted. Dinners at midnight, lunches on the run, early morning commutes—whether by train or even by bicycle, coffee grabbed with friends, lots of cell phones, text messages, and emails. When do you ever rest? I appreciate you allowing me to tag along for this fast ride. I learned so much from you and your friends and coworkers.

Thank you to all the many, many people who allowed me to ask questions and who were willing to answer with clarity and truth. Although most were young women, many men gave advice and perspectives that painted a picture of the culture in a more clear and concrete way. That was great.

A special thank you to all of the hundreds of twentysomething girls that I have had the blessing of watching and being a part of their lives since their early grammar school years. I have watched you grow and seen the truth of the fact that "you are who you are becoming." Keep growing. You are awesome.

None of this would be possible without New Hope Publishers. I am thankful for a publishing company that is willing to run with all of my ideas. I am certain that at times they would love for me to "slow down," but life is fast and I just seem to get and stay in the middle of it. Thank you to Rebecca England, my editor, who can take all my words and condense them just a little to fit the format of the book. You have such a gift with words and I appreciate your input into my books. Thank you, Tara Miler, my marketing director. You let me speak my ideas and never discourage me from writing what "just comes up." You have such a wonderful eye for detail. Thank you for using your gifts to enhance my gift of writing to its highest potential. Tamzen Benfield, what a blessing you are to help with this manuscript. Your copyediting allowed me to be more creative. That gave me so much time to write even more. And a thank you to all who promote, edit, print, and produce. This is very much a group effort.

Allene and Foots Parnell gave me an absolutely wonderful, fabulous computer after the homegoing of their beautiful twentysomething daughter, Carleton Benners Parnell. I think of her every time my hands touch the keyboard. With thanksgiving for her life—for one who truly knew the reality of the fact that life is not a do-over nor a dress rehearsal.

To God be the glory.

introduction

Quarter-Life
Crisis

"Life hurts! Twenties generation
finds life a big bummer."
—*Denver Post*, January 6, 2003

The *Denver Post* article went on to say, "College degrees, independence and financial autonomy are not cutting it anymore for twentysomethings. Many recent grads feel the world owes them a good
job, a great salary and all the trimmings. If twentysomethings are
not bestowed with their heart's desire, they say depression, self-
loathing and crisis may soon follow. This period, dubbed 'Quarter-
Life Crisis,' is the time after college graduation when reality sets in.
Life, work, broken relationships and bills. Lots of bills, including the
hefty car insurance premiums your parents paid while you were
studying. Welcome to the real world of interviews and no jobs. If
you get work, it's a world where co-workers have time only for
babies and carpooling instead of gossip and shopping" (*The Denver
Post*, January 6, 2003).

For over 30 years I have served as the founder and director of Community Ministry for Girls, a faith-based, service-oriented inter-denominational Bible study program for girls. This began in Birmingham, Alabama, with 12 girls attending the first meeting. Since that time, in Birmingham alone more than 3,500 girls have begun the program, which they enter during their fifth-grade year and remain a part of until their graduation from high school. As the girls left for college, I received many letters telling of the joys, adventures, and disasters of college life. Many of these are recorded in *Letters from Campus: College Girls' Insights for High School Graduates*, which was released in the spring of 2003. As I began the enormous task of tracking these girls down in order to receive permission to print their thoughts, many approached me with the comment, "You prepared us for junior high, high school, and college, but *no one* prepared us for the 'real world.' Help!"

Now, an even more monumental project loomed—how could I gather thoughts on the "real world" from young women who were literally all over planet earth? I needed lots of help. I wrote a letter asking for truth about life past college, and began to distribute them to girls that I knew personally. They in turn, passed the letters to their friends and these friends responded in kind. This book represents the written thoughts from nearly 150 graduates, representing more than 90 colleges, universities, graduate schools, and seminaries. Their names are recorded in the back of this book with a list of the schools represented. Many grew up in Community Ministry for Girls, but a large number are new friends that I look forward to meeting one day and thanking in person for sharing their perspectives on the "real world."

In the letter, I asked, "Just write whatever comes up when you think about life after graduation. Don't think too hard. This is not an academic exercise. I want your heart. What you say will remain anonymous. Only your age will appear beside your comments.

Think—what do you wish someone had told you about the 'real world' before you became a part of it?"

While almost 150 young women between the ages of 21 and 29 responded in writing, I had opportunities to speak with several hundred more and glean from them impressions, facts, and stories about their "real world" struggles and adventures. More times than I can recall, I heard the words, "Oh yes, I can tell you about the 'real world.'" And so, as I became an eager observer of the quarter-life cultures of Washington DC and New York City, I listened with my head but more deeply with my heart.

> When looking back now, there are so many things I wish someone had told me before entering the real world. The first of such advice is that once you enter the real world, you can't leave. So with that said, here are a few of the pieces of wisdom I have gleaned over the years . . .
>
> —Age 28

> Graduation from college and entering the real world is a dream we have all looked forward to and worked hard to obtain. It's easy to think that with enough education, we will surely be prepared for what lies ahead. Unfortunately, knowledge and wisdom are not enough to make one fully ready for life after college! I have come to understand that we learn life's most important lessons in the classroom of experience.
>
> —Age 25

> I really feel like the transition from college to the real world is so much harder than the transition was to college. And it is true that no one ever really tells you how to deal with it. It is just assumed you graduate and get a job and you are supposed to be happy about it and ready for it, but it just isn't that way.

It's really a whole new time of learning and growing that wasn't possible when we lived in the little college bubble.

—Age 26

Leaving college and entering the real world are going to be some of the best times, yet also the loneliest times. To me, it's kind of like entering your freshman year all over again. You will find that you and your friends from college will soon all part separate ways to pursue a career, explore another part of the country, or further their education. Many will struggle with the decision of where to live. Know that it is normal to go through this. We all want some sort of sign to come before us to ensure us that we've made the right decision. But remember this—most choices aren't permanent. You can correct your mistakes!

—Age 26

The real world really is not that bad. As a matter of fact, it is very exciting! I was just not prepared for how drastic the transition would be. No one had prepared me for the issues and challenges that I would face. When I realized what it was going to be like, I was able to adapt to the new environment. Expectations are so important. There are so many books about expectations for college, marriage, parenting, and a plethora of other topics. Why is there not more information about the transition from college to the real world? It has been the hardest transition that I have faced in my life (marriage was a breeze compared to the real world). If I had realized that everyone else was feeling the same way, it would not have been as lonely. Knowing that Christ was by my side was a tremendous help because He was one of the few friends that I had near me.

The Bible verse that helped me most was: "Cast all your anxiety on him because he cares for you" (1 Peter 5:7).

—Age 28

I want to begin by telling you how awesome and how real God is. God is the way, and without God, nothing will be lasting. "Unless the Lord builds the house, its builders labor in vain" (Psalm 127:1). This is so true. I think that lots of young people feel as if they are lost. I have heard people refer to us as a lost generation. People talk about us having a quarter-life crisis. This can be avoided, and, in fact, it is God's perfect destiny for us to know Him and to live in the fullness of His life. There is no need for us to feel lost and confused when God has a purpose and a plan for us, a future and a destiny (Jeremiah 29:11).

—Age 24

The Bible can give comfort and encouragement to twentysomethings facing the real world. God clearly wants the best for you. "For I know the plans I have for you,' declares the Lord, 'plans to prosper you and not to harm you, plans to give you hope and a future" (Jeremiah 29:11). Join with me as we explore the many paths taken on this journey toward your future—the transition period from college to a life of different proportions—the "real world."

one

Transition from College to the "Real World"

For years, I trained for and ran marathons. Although the 26.2-mile run was never easy for me personally, the training part was even more difficult. At times it seemed never ending. And after running up to 20 miles at a time, the rewards were water, food, a shower, and a collapse on the sofa. As I ran with my body screaming, "Stop!" I would repeat this little saying: "Inch by inch, life's a cinch. Yard by yard, it's always hard."

I needed to just put one foot in front of the other and keep going. The transition from college to the "real world" often means simply doing the next thing. But what is that thing? What do I do? What is the next step?

No Certain Next Step

I have heard it said quite often lately about life after college that "it is the first time in a person's life that there is no certain next step." Growing up, we go from one stage to the next, elementary to junior high to high school to college, and it is comfortable and safe and predictable. But college ends, and for the first time it is our turn to make a choice as to what our next step will be. Graduate school? Traveling? Service or missions work? Job? I realized that there were many, many doors opened to me, but going through one would close all the others (at least for now). As I began to develop my plan, my next step, I involved God, but I certainly was not letting Him be the guide. So, as my plan began to crumble, I felt failure and loneliness. It was only months later that I could look back and see that His ways were truly better for me.

—Age 24

Several Different Jobs

I have been out of college for about three years now. I always felt pressured to know exactly what I wanted to do with my life right after college. But the thing is, you don't need to know. I majored in fashion retailing, and my first job post-college was at a huge financial corporation. It took me about two years to realize that the job was not my niche. But I don't regret it, because I learned so much about business. I have been through several different jobs since then, and I think that you cannot put a time constraint on finding what you want to do. All your jobs will be learning experiences, and all will be a source of knowledge. My advice is not to stress yourself out over it. You don't have to find your niche in life the moment you leave college. You'll learn what you want as a result of finding what you don't want!

—Age 25

For many, facing the unknown world of adulthood is the hardest part of leaving college. The greatest comfort is the fact that although no one really knows their future, it is possible to know the One who does know every single detail of our lives. Remember, Psalm 139:16 says, "All the days ordained for me were written in your book before one of them came to be."

God Always Goes Before You

I had an awesome experience in college. When you graduate, you are in for a lot of change, and it can be shocking. However, you can rely on the fact that God always goes before you and prepares a place for you. I think it is difficult when you graduate and feel that you are supposed to know your place in this world immediately and fit right in. You don't. People our age have had exposure to so many things and so many options; this is one way that the devil can send even more confusion to us. God is sovereign, though, which is a huge deal, and I am learning to appreciate that more and more. What sovereign means is that no matter what we do or how hard we try, God's plan will prevail and work and set our destiny. God is above all things.

—Age 24

Learning to Just Relax

My 25th year was one of great self-discovery and contentment. After years of believing I should always be on the go, scrambling after success, I have learned to just relax. I am concentrating on growing closer to God and listening to His call and direction. Things can seem so complicated, but really, they're very simple. I've learned that all I really have to do is live, just be, just enjoy life, be close to God, listen, and wait. I know now how to enjoy myself: have a cup of tea, say a prayer, work a crossword puzzle, read a book, and just be myself. I don't feel that I have to be doing something all the time or that I need to be seeing people or meeting guys. I don't need to be invited to everything. I have all I need. It's funny that it is such a great epiphany, but perhaps others will experience the same thing. We are given everything that we need. I learned to just lean on Jesus.

—Age 25

Network of Friends

Between work and travel, I don't have time to cultivate friendships like I've been used to having. In college, there was always a group. Whether it was classmates or sorority sisters, people were always there. It doesn't seem to be the case post-college. There are more people around, that's for sure, but finding those with whom you mesh well is not always easy.

—Age 24

Coping with Hard Times

I've had trouble believing that I'm supposed to be in this place at this time. I've been so unhappy here that I wonder why God would put me into this situation. Sometimes amid all the noise up here and all the things going on, I don't hear His voice, and I feel like I don't have any direction. I wasn't prepared for the sheer exhaustion, mentally and physically, that comes at the end of each workday. I just want to curl up and let God put His arms around me. I think if I could just get myself out of the way and let God do His thing that He would direct me to areas of work I would enjoy, and lead me to people who will have positive influences on me. Although I know deep down that things will work out just as He plans, I just can't seem to figure out why we have to go through the hard times.

—Age 24

Advice for Twentysomething Living

Obtain a healthy balance of work and play. If you work too much, you can easily get burned out, frustrated, or depressed. And if you play too much, your job can be put on the line; promotions or progress in your career are significantly compromised. A good balance is important.

—Age 25

· Keep in touch with your true friends. You begin to realize what a blessing they are.
· We are not given a "spirit of timidity," so don't be afraid to stand for Jesus in the workplace.
· Find your niche and check your spiritual growth often— the "real world" can stunt growth.
· Find contentment quickly in Christ because the "real world" always threatens contentment!

—Age 28

I would encourage you today to:
1. Pursue your passions. What has God laid on your heart? Use your story to give to others. (If not in the workplace, then with your hobbies and free time)
2. Find heart friends who care about your life and are also headed towards God.
3. Plug into a God-glorifying church where you can serve with your gifts and experience community in worship.
4. Journal the feelings of your soul. This practice will build your faith and serve as a testimony to others.
5. Look for other women who need to know Jesus.
6. Pray for a mentor and seek out women who live out God's dreams.

—Age 27

Lessons we learn in life are often only apparent long after we've learned them. The years right after college seem more packed with these life lessons than even the college years. Here are a few lessons of mine from college and beyond.

1. Our parents' intentions are right, but their logic might be completely different. Dig deeper when you disagree.
2. Don't be afraid to make a change in (or out of!) a dating relationship. Dating should be fun the majority of the time. If it causes more stress than fun, something is wrong!
3. Stand up for yourself. At this point in life, if something feels wrong to you, chances are it *is* wrong for you!
4. Hoping something will happen won't make it happen.
5. Everyone has something to say. Why not be the listener this time?
6. Learn from the mistakes of others. Watch the aftereffects closely and be thankful *you* don't have to go through them.
7. What are you passionate about? Passion makes us who we are, and when we have a grip on that, we are two steps ahead of most.
8. Don't be ashamed of who you are.
9. Patience is a virtue. I was told this at an early age but didn't learn it until recently. Life's lessons aren't always fun to go through, but patience will bring the punch line.

—Age 22

My advice to college graduates who are entering the real world is this: never be ashamed of who you are or your heritage. Stick to your beliefs in a world that desperately needs strong, godly women. Be genuine and real and do all you can to rid yourself of all hypocrisy. The real world is looking for REAL people.

—Age 26

two

The Real World Is Looking for REAL People

The people of the world look for reality and happiness in wealth, thrills, conquest, religion, education and power. In and of themselves, these things are not wrong. The main problem with these things is that they are temporary. There is no lasting power in the things of the world. All will vanish. "The world and its desires pass away, but the man who does the will of God lives forever" (1 John 2:17).

Only two things will last forever—the Word of God and the souls of men. Life that is real, life that is satisfying, comes from a deep, personal, love relationship with Jesus Christ.

"That which was from the beginning, which we have heard, which we have seen with our eyes, which we have looked at and our hands have touched—this we proclaim concerning the Word of life. The life appeared; we have seen it and testify to it, and we proclaim to you the eternal life, which was with the Father and has appeared to us. We proclaim to you what we have seen and heard, so that you also may have fellowship with us. And our fellowship is with the Father and with His Son, Jesus Christ. We write this to make our joy complete."

—1 John 1:1–4

These are facts about this "real" life. It is openly revealed. We do not have to search for it. It is not hidden. God has revealed himself to us in His creation. He has given us the Bible, which is the living Word of God. And most importantly, God has given his Son, Jesus Christ. Christ reveals the mind and heart of God. He is the living means of communication between God and men. To know Jesus Christ is to know God. Jesus is the Son of God. He is the complete and final revelation of God to men.

Real life is experienced only after we have believed the gospel, put our trust in Christ, and been born of God. "Everyone who believes that Jesus is the Christ is born of God" (1 John 5:1a).

As the Holy Spirit controls the lives of believers, their lives begin to reflect more and more of Jesus. They do not practice sin as a habit. Their lives are righteous although not perfect. They love God, and they love and respect each other because of His love. The world's system has less of a hold on them, which means that the believer may be going against what is popular, politically correct, or comfortable. Because of this, the world may hate them. "Do not be surprised, my brothers, if the world hates you" (1 John 3:13). This may be difficult at times, but instead of being swept off balance in the "real" world, those who know who they are in Christ can be overcomers.

The "real" life is meant to be shared with the "real" world. We share our own spiritual experiences with others by the lives we live and the words we speak. As we share the deep places of our hearts and become vulnerable, others are given the freedom to respond in kind. And friendships are begun on deep levels, which is God's answer to a lonely life. Joy is Christ's answer to an empty life. Life that is real produces joy that is real. And remember, " . . . no one will take away your joy" (John 16:22).

Story of a Goody-Goody

If you were to read the biography of my life, only one thing would come to mind . . . "what a goody-goody!" I have never done anything wild, never been a drinker, never smoked, or had premarital sex. I made great grades and was in church every time the doors were open (my dad was in the ministry).

I attended the same small, private, Christian school from kindergarten through twelfth grade, and I went to a small Christian college. When the day came to graduate, anxiety came along with it. Everything in my life had been small—small elementary and high school and small college. Now it was time to enter the real world . . . the real world with a real job, with real people who did not believe like I did. What if they didn't accept me? I didn't want to change who I was, but what if I had to change in order to find a job? Or to just fit in? These are all the thoughts that flooded my sheltered little mind.

Well, God has a sense of humor! After my "small" life, I got a job with one of the largest employers in Birmingham! I was nervous about my goody-goody past being a hindrance to me, but God kept telling me to just be myself—to be REAL and genuine in a world that has had its fill of counterfeit people.

As I started my job, I made a promise to myself to stick to my faith, my morals, and my God. I know that if I stick to Him, He'll stick to me! And although I thought that people in the "real" world would make fun of me or not accept me for who I am, I have learned that they truly respect my beliefs, my Christian lifestyle, and even my innocence and naïveté.

—Age 26

Stick to It!

If I gave any advice about entering the real world after college, it would be to know who you are, what you believe, and stick to it. You are going to be thrown into all kinds of groups. I think I noticed this most in the working world. You have no control over who your co-workers are going to be. You are thrown with people from all walks of life and all different backgrounds. You are put together to work together, which is not always easy. In addition, because you are young, you are going to be tested even that much more. Remember who you are, what you believe, and stick to it. Don't get caught up in tacky water cooler conversations just to fit in. People in the real world will like you because of who you are. Be yourself.

—Age 27

New Friends Can Lead Astray

All through college I had my group of friends. For the most part we were just alike, and the differences that we had, we totally accepted in each other. Then I graduated, married, moved away, and began graduate school. I had a lot of changes in a very short time. The hardest thing to get used to was not having my friends beside me every day. I had to make new friends and learn not to put pressure on my husband to fill these new voids. I did make a new group of friends, but they were completely opposite of the sheltered circle I had left behind. My new friends were a bit crazier— and that started to change me. I started feeling as if I didn't really need God as much.

I can remember sitting with my new girlfriends and they were talking about boyfriends and different experiences with them. I revealed to them that my husband and I had waited until marriage to have sex. They could not believe this about me. I was instantly embarrassed about something that earlier had meant something to me! I was totally forgetting who I was and doubting my values. I learned so much the first couple of years out of college. While I was going through it, though, it was confusing and lonely at times. It is hard when you are on your own and it is easy to forget important things about yourself. My advice is: hang on to who you really are, stay true to yourself, and the most important person's opinion to you should be Jesus'.

—Age 28

Building Blocks for Life

"What is it that someone never told me about the real world?" I don't think I have a concrete answer for that question because I want to mention what didn't need to be told. My values have been the building blocks to a happy, successful marriage and life. My parents and other influential adults never had to teach me these values. I learned by example. Because I grew up in Christian home and spent rewarding time in Bible study, I knew that I would be ready for the real world. I knew the importance of quiet times, prayer, hard and rewarding work, self-pride, love, and many other attributes that make me happy to be who I am today. These values were so important as I left the innocent atmosphere of college, into a new job and a new life as a wife.

The one thing that no one ever told me about the real world wasn't necessary. It was already sewed deep into my

heart without words ever directly spoken. Be proud of who
you are, what you've learned, and what you can become.

—Age 26

The real life involves all of our personality. We were made in God's image in mind, heart and will. A Spirit-controlled mind knows and understands truth. A Spirit-controlled heart feels love, and a Spirit-controlled will draws us to obedience.

Real people know who they are in Christ and have experienced this confidence firsthand, which gives even more confidence to stand and be who they are. That's called authenticity! And that leads to a life filled with serenity and contentment.

three

Finding Contentment

The transition from college to the "real world" can be difficult, but I am reminded of the quote I display on my refrigerator as a reminder to myself: "Contentment: Understanding that if I am not satisfied with what I have, I will never be satisfied with what I want."

The secret of contentment is found in the way we look at something. Proverbs 23:7 teaches us: "for as he thinks within himself, so he is." There are many thieves that can rob us of our joy, but there is great hope for the Christian. We can choose joy!

Every Christian should take advantage of joy—a product of being filled with God's Holy Spirit. Joy is the deep settled confidence that God is in control, and it leads to peace of mind and deep contentment. Peace of mind is a quality we all desire. Everyone searches for this. Relationships, wealth, worldly success, drugs, alcohol, popularity, etc. will never fill the void that was meant to be filled by God alone.

Comparing ourselves to others, for whatever reason, will always lead to the wrong path of thought. No two people or situations are ever alike. There is danger in feeling superior as well as inferior. But when you trust that God has made you and led you to the place where you are, you can experience contentment.

When we trust God, we might not always get what we want. However, we can trust that God will always provide our needs. Why do things happen or not happen in a certain way? We may never have the answers this side of heaven. However, we can always rest assured that God sees the "big picture" and is concerned about all the details of our lives..

Meet My Neighbors . . . the Joneses

You know the saying "keeping up with the Joneses"? Why do they always seem to live right next door to us? Actually, they aren't stalking us. We are following them! There is always one thing (or several things) "they" have that we feel would make us much happier. Who are the Joneses, anyway? Are they the couple that has a new baby, the friend who got the best job after graduating, or the girl dating the coolest guy? Whatever it may be that we desire to have, jealousy eats us up. We gradually become less and less content, and as a result our joy is gone.

Our Biblical friend, Paul, is a good example of a man who learned contentment and joy. Here's someone who had it all, including family, wealth, an excellent education, and prestige. However, he had no joy. It wasn't until he sacrificed everything for the gospel that he found joy in Christ. The man is writing a letter from jail stating that no matter what situation he is in, he has learned to be content (Philippians 4:11-12). Wow!

When we start comparing ourselves to the Joneses, we start desiring more and thinking we have less. Take time to write down all the things that you are grateful for and praise the Lord for them. And remember . . . somebody somewhere considers you one of the Joneses!

—Age 28

Choose Joy

Choose God, choose joy: it's an action. Each experience in the "real" world will be different, and God must be your constant in order to make it through. A life you orchestrate will be a disaster. A life He orchestrates will be a delight! Suffering, sadness, and trials are not bad but are an opportunity to grow. They only last for a season.

—Age 22

Trust the Waiting Time

I believe one of the most difficult things for young women right out of college is the high expectations that they put on themselves. As you watch your roommate plan her fairytale wedding or get hired for her dream job, you begin to wonder when your life will become the exciting adventure you always thought it would be. Comparing yourself to others will only lead to disappointment and poor decisions. There is no magic time when certain events should happen in your life. Slowing down and waiting for the right timing is so difficult to do when you want everything to happen right away. Trust that waiting will bring what is best for you, whether it is a job, a relationship, or any other meaningful experience.

—Age 30

A Black Hole

When I graduated from college, I was so excited about being on my own. The prospects of my own apartment and a corporate job were very exciting. I was ready to make my mark on the world. God had blessed me in my life, so I knew that great things lay ahead. Little did I know that I would be completely depressed and discouraged after a month of being out in the real world.

I was in a new city. How would I find my way around? Would I find a church where I felt like I belonged? Where would I get my hair cut? Who would be a good doctor? How would I make new friends?

I started my first job in January, and the only light of day I saw was on the 10-minute drive into work every morning. It was dark every day when I left work. I was so overwhelmed with the amount of time I spent at work each day. No more two-hour breaks in the afternoon to run errands or hang out with friends. When I did get off work, everywhere I needed to go was closed. Running errands became a major challenge. So I fell into the mindless routine of getting up, going to work, coming home, eating dinner, and going to bed. The only good thing was that I did not have to do any homework at night!

The work environment was a rude awakening because I was the low man on the totem pole with no credibility. I had not yet built a reputation of being responsible and dependable. If I made a mistake at work, everyone was very quick and blunt in pointing it out. Unlike in college when you had a bad class and you knew it would be over in a matter of weeks, I had no idea how long I would be stuck in this job. I felt like I was thrust into this black hole.

I also felt very isolated from all of my friends. I was used to being around them all the time. Now, I did not even know what was going on with them. I felt like everyone else was having good times while I slaved away at my entry-level job.

It took several months to adjust to this new routine, but fortunately there was a light at the end of the tunnel. God was faithful to see me through this difficult transition. After about six months, I began to get the hang of it. Eventually, I learned to manage my time better. I took one lunch a week to run errands. My friends and I committed to get together at least one night a month. I became involved in a Bible study that gave me weekly fellowship with other Christian women. Little by little, I started making the most of my time away from work. Getting involved in community groups and a church gave me a sense that this big, new city was becoming home. And as time went by, I was able to build some respect from my coworkers based on the work I had done.

—Age 28

Long-Distance Relationship

Contentment is a hard lesson to learn. My struggle actually began before college. I couldn't wait to go to college and finally be "on my own." In college, I couldn't wait until classes were over for a break. Then, I couldn't wait to get to the camp I was working at that summer. I was looking to the next thing in my life so much that I had a hard time living in the present. I found myself discouraged, discontent, ignoring what God had blessed me with: great friends, a great school, a great sorority . . . overall, great everything.

After my freshman year in college, God allowed me to meet the guy I would one day marry. The only catch was that he went to school in Arkansas and was from Louisiana. I was going to school in Alabama and was from Tennessee. In fact, when we first met, I was only home for two weeks before I left to work at a camp for the whole summer. We felt God telling us pretty quickly in our relationship that we would marry. We only saw each other once a month, basically dating over the phone. Our phone bills were astronomical! That pattern continued for the rest of our three-year, long-distance relationship.

I found myself living only for those phone calls and short weekends that we got to see each other. All the other weekends that we were separated I felt depressed. I couldn't wait to get engaged and then I couldn't wait until we got married. Time just couldn't move fast enough. I felt worse when I saw my friends dating guys who went to school with us. My life was full of discontentment. Why did we have to be so far apart? Why couldn't we have met later and not have had to wait so long to get married? Was this God's cruel way of teaching us patience? It seemed like all I did was complain about the wishing, waiting, and wanting.

I look back now and see how much time I wasted being discontent in my circumstances. But, it's not the circumstances that should control our joy and contentment, it's who we place our trust in—God. He knows what we need for each time and season of our life. He gives us exactly what we can handle for that particular time.

Here's a hard truth. When we focus on what we don't have, we're essentially missing the blessings of life that God has set out for us. So here's your plan of action. Trust in God, rest in His plan, and rejoice in what He's given you at the time. I promise that your list of positives will far outweigh your list of negatives if you honestly evaluate your life in light of God's plan and goodness for you.

—Age 25

Trials Are Gifts

God is currently using my circumstances—moving to a new city, beginning my first real job—to increase my dependence and trust in Him. Some days, I am completely sure that the Lord is working, and some days I doubt and wonder what I am doing here. But I have learned to trust that this is where the Lord has directed me and to trust His plans for me. I hold onto the truth that the trials of this life are *gifts* to produce perseverance and our ultimate satisfaction. I realize that if there were any other place that would be better for me and my growth in the Lord—whether in the realm of marriage, my job, or where I live—I would be there.

The Lord has also taught me to not wallow in discontentment and worry, but to remember His faithfulness in the past and for the future. Looking back, some things that I felt were changes in my situation were really changes in my attitude regarding the situation. All of this has given me a new hope and peace that the Lord's plans, regardless of whether I think they are good or not, will prosper me and give me hope and a future.

—Age 23

Choose Christ

Whoever coined the phrase "don't worry—be happy" obviously wasn't a woman living with the demands of today. How do we make sure "the peace of God . . . will guard your hearts and your minds" (Philippians 4:7)? We must realize that *everything* in life—every relationship, every hardship, trial, joy, success, every detail—ultimately reverts back to God and our personal relationship with Him. Despite our pleas, tears, demands (yelling, kicking or screaming!), we cannot control other people, we cannot control our circumstances, and we most definitely cannot control God! But we are responsible for our own hearts, minds, motives, and attitudes. It is how we react in hard times and trials that reveals our true character and knowledge of God. God has given us choices. Choose to focus on your own heart instead of worrying about everyone else's. Choose Christ. Always choose to follow hard after Him. This is the true secret to happiness and contentment.

—Age 25

Making the Most of Being Single

four

So you want to get married, but here you are at 24, 27, or even 30 and you're not. How do you feel? Resentful, frustrated, discouraged, confused, or discontent? Most women desire to be married, and that is completely all right. But reality is that for a variety of reasons, some women won't marry.

Marriage was created by God, and it is good. Man and woman were created by God to complement each other. She was to be his fulfillment and he was also to be hers. But when sin entered the garden, things went wrong for Adam and Eve. Men and women deserted God's plans and sought to run their own lives in the fashion they desired. Sin, disease, and twisted personalities resulted. Women of the twenty-first century now face a multitude of questions that Eve never dreamed of. Many questions must be answered:

Is marriage the only answer?

Is marriage the best answer?

Is marriage the best answer for you?

What if marriage is not a part of the plan for your life or at least not for this time of your life? How can this be handled so that life will have real fulfillment and excitement? Is there a full, rich life apart from marriage? Why do you want to get married? Who are you and what does God envision for you? What is His plan? What is His timing?

Do It All!

The years just after graduating from college have been the hardest time and yet a time of deep growth and enjoyment of life. It has been a time for me to do it all! Life is full of great single friends and my wonderful family. My main advice to girls who are just graduating is to enjoy this time—you are open to a world of opportunities. Each day I can choose to either "indulge" and live for myself, or invest my time and freedom for the good of many other people. I began to realize that only in this situation will I have the flexibility in life to do so many things and give to the "body of Christ," the church. It's all about balance. I continue to enjoy this time in my life and be all there!

—Age 26

Delightful Freedom

My closest friends and I have loved our "single years" that followed college. I had been completely convinced that the only option for me was to marry just before college gradua-tion, but I was pleasantly surprised to discover a different plan awaited me. After a couple of different jobs in different cities, I began to realize the delightful freedom that was granted me! Many a road trip, a new friendship, and an increased understanding of who I am have come as a result of these single years.

I share this not to say that one option is better than the other—marriage or singleness—but to give testimony to the truth of God's Word in a believer's life. Proverbs 21:2 teaches us that "All a man's ways seem right to him, but the Lord weighs the heart." I want to go God's way, rather than my own. For as long as I live on earth, I have asked the Lord to increasingly make His Word a reality in my life, that my hope would rest in Him. Let me encourage you to seek contentment now.

And finally, *travel if you are single*—it's much more affordable when you're paying for one!

—Age 27

Wanting Someone Else's Life

Three months after I moved to a new city and a new life, my younger sister, a senior in college, got engaged. At that point, I realized she had gotten the life I had always wanted. I had wanted to meet my husband in college, get engaged as a senior, and married after graduation. Why had that not happened to me? My reaction wasn't one of anger, but rather confusion. I questioned God. "Lord, I want to follow Your will. Why am I miserable? Why am I alone? Do You care about me?"

This was my breaking point. I crashed. I was broken, and God was the only one who could fix me. God has a way of bringing us to our knees. He wanted to begin a love affair with me. He wants to become the Lord of my life.

Now that I am "alone," away from the *distractions* of friends, family, and familiarity, God is beginning to show me who I really am. I now see that I have been insecure, and that I have gotten my self-worth from others. Wanting people to like me is okay, but not when my self-confidence and identity depend upon it. My identity should come from God alone.

God is also teaching me that His plan for my life is unique. I can't compare my life and circumstances to others—even my sister and friends. Sometimes I still throw pity parties for myself. But the Lord is teaching me to embrace this time in my life. Singleness affords me the time to reach out for God's Kingdom in ways that will become impossible once I am married. Singleness allows me the time to truly examine my heart in the purest form, to see what is good and what is ugly, to allow God to cleanse it without dragging another person through the process with me. Above all, singleness is a gift as marriage is a gift. If I see the gift of singleness as less than the gift of marriage, then I am deceived. I see myself as an unanchored vessel ready to go wherever He leads. Most importantly, this time is teaching me to become completely secure in the fact that I am God's child, and my identity lies in being His daughter.

—Age 24

Don't Be Anxious

God has been teaching me much about *contentment* over the past few years. After graduating from college, I was anxious to get married and have a family. I found myself always looking forward to the next phase or stage in life. God really began teaching me what it meant to be content and to be satisfied where He had me. I want to be living in the present and not wishing it away by focusing on the next stage. This realization has brought much peace, satisfaction, and happiness to my life.

The Lord has also been teaching me about what it means to not be anxious about the future. It is an amazing comfort to know that we can trust Him at all times. He is faithful, and He alone is my security. "Praise be to the Lord, for he showed his wonderful love to me when I was in a besieged city" (Psalm 31:21). I love the phase of life that I am in right now. I am taking advantage of the fact that I am single, which enables me to travel and to do many things that I enjoy. I feel extremely blessed to have this opportunity.

—Age 27

How important to realize that there is more to life than marriage. Don't just wait around for it to happen. Instead, find attractive niches for yourself and extend your personality in many different directions. Don't just fill in the time until marriage comes along. This is the time for developing your talents and increasing your skills and abilities. God does not hand out talents haphazardly, and whatever yours is, it's both your privilege and your responsibility to use it as God directs.

Many times God waits until we stop shouting to Him and clutching with our own desires concerning marriage. A tight hold may strangle your own spirit, causing you to be much less than God intended for you to be. Are you able to let go and say to God, "I leave it up to You. If You really want me to, I am willing to accept singleness"?

Have you thought about the fact that those who are married are often envious of those who are single? Marrieds often see singles as able to spend money on clothes, travel, a new car, or expanded study, while they are tied down with diapers and laundry. Balance is key. Both viewpoints can become extreme. But do enjoy your freedom. Develop and grow as an individual. Make the most of the moment. All we have is today. Squeeze enjoyment from every day. Treasure friendships. Cultivate appreciation of the intrinsic value of now, however much you may long for tomorrow.

Dating Relationships

five

Most twentysomethings are interested in dating and love. This can be a wonderful adventure for some, but for others a time of frustration, discouragement, or depression. Struggles with sexual temptations can cause discouragement. One girl might like a special person who doesn't even know that she exists. Others may say, "Dating? What's that?" Whatever the case, God has a special design for dating that will truly make us happy.

The Bible does not speak specifically about dating. In fact, marriages were arranged by families during Bible times. Young women would never have been allowed to make the choice of whom they wanted to spend time with and certainly unmarried men and women did not spend time together alone. However, God's Word gives standards and guidelines for having honorable relationships with those of the opposite sex. Dating provides a time for a friendship to grow between a man and woman, which often leads to engagement and marriage. God's desire is that we let Him control this area of our lives. He wants our entire dating life as well as future marriage plans. Wow! That's difficult. Why is it that we as human beings find it easy to trust God with so many areas of our lives—but when it comes to a relationship the reins get pulled in tightly? We think, *God can't possibly know what's best for me when it comes to a man.*

Listen to the journey of a 22-year-old woman as she sought her own dating path for a season only to find that God held the better plan.

Is the Wrong Boyfriend Better Than None?

At summer camp my way of thinking about dating relationships was strongly challenged. The speaker asked each of us to list the characteristics we desired our date or mate to possess. I had never even thought about this before—and I was in a dating relationship! My list included: good looking (of course), a leader by example, a servant, someone who respects others, listens to and seeks God everyday . . . my list went on and on. When I was finished, I thought—*How in the world am I even to find someone like this? I'm too picky!*

After camp, I went home. When the list popped into my mind, I shoved it back. I remained in the same relationship. I was compromising what God wanted for me. I compromised my beliefs about remaining sexually pure before marriage. I compromised my beliefs of dating a type of guy that God had intended for me. My parents and friends were not supportive, and I just ignored signs from the Lord. The longer I ignored them, the worse things became. God was asking me to obey Him and trust Him that I deserved something better. But I was just too comfortable where I was and I didn't want to risk anything. I refused to listen and I was trapped in my own misery. So what did I do about this? Nothing. I thought that's how life was supposed to be, just mediocre. My relationship with God was mediocre. Everything was mediocre because I did not have enough faith to trust God.

But God had plans to change my life. My boyfriend broke up with me—which devastated me at the time. But God continued to show me as time went on how this is what He wanted for me. I learned so much about truly being a servant and I began renewing my relationship with God.

I had been dependent on my boyfriend for so long that I didn't know what to do now that he was gone. Every day I would spend at least an hour praying and studying God's Word trying to find direction for my life. I became a leader of a girls' discipleship group, spent more time with friends, and built trust again with my family. I began to become more dependent on God and I realized that He did have a perfect plan for me even if I didn't know what it was.

Later I met another man. And guess what? He was everything on my list of characteristics and even more. God knew what I needed and He gave it to me regardless of my past. He has provided for me in ways I could never have imagined.

—Age 22

Unanswered Prayer

I have learned firsthand the blessing of unanswered prayer. A three-year courtship, proposal, engagement ring, and wedding plans ended abruptly with a cancelled wedding. My heart was broken, dreams dashed, and my life deeply altered. I had been so certain that marrying this man was the plan God had for me. But as always, His plans were much better. In that time of despair, my relationship with God deepened in ways I could never have fathomed. As I lay on my face before

Him asking why, as I sought His will, I found Him. The more I knew Him, the deeper my trust grew. Now I don't ask why, I just move over and let Him lead. Oh, yes, God's plans are best and I know as I wait in eager anticipation for my wedding day. As I write, there are only two more months until I become one with the man God intended for me—His very best!

—Age 28

There is no way to have truly successful dating relationship without Jesus in complete control. Remember, we should "Seek first his kingdom and his righteousness, and all these things will be given to you as well" (Matthew 6:33). As wonderful as any man is, he was not designed to meet the deepest needs of a woman's heart. It's easy to cling to a person or relationship when God desires that we cling to Him. Can you say to God with the psalmist: "earth has nothing I desire besides you. My flesh and my heart may fail, but God is the strength of my heart and my portion forever" (Psalm 73:25–26)?

You may have periods of panic, thinking, *God must have forgotten me*, or fearing that God is going to give you a less-than-wonderful date and husband. Freedom comes when we are able to say to God—"I am willing for whatever You want for me."

Graduation, Then Marriage?

When I graduated from college, I was dating a guy who had been one of my close friends throughout the past 4 years. We had been dating about 4 months when we graduated. It seemed like the natural next step would be to get married. I found myself thinking that would be our next step, although it didn't really excite me. That's when I realized something was wrong and we broke up. I grew up thinking that you go to college to find your husband, so I limited myself to thinking that way. And I feared that if I didn't find my husband at college, I would never find him. But the fear of being alone should never be the driving force in a relationship. It has been cool since college to see how the Lord has woven guys into my life in unexpected ways. I get sad when I see people settling for less than God's best for them for fear that they will be alone. But it isn't by any means the end of the world to graduate from college without a boyfriend or husband!

—Age 26

Being older gave me the maturity to see that the person God has chosen for me to marry might not look exactly as I had pictured in my mind, or might not be who I *thought* others expected me to marry. Life experience has given me the ability to see through expectations to reality, which has proven to be far greater than anything I could have imagined!

—Age 28

What are the right reasons and motives for dating? Relationships help us to grow as individuals. We learn more about who we are, discover our strengths and weaknesses. We learn more about giving vs. taking—how to be less selfish. Dating provides a time for encouragement and ultimately prepares us for marriage. It helps us to see personality traits that best match or complement our own. It goes without saying that the person you marry will be one of the persons you dated, which adds an important perspective to *whom* you go out with.

You Decide

As for dating—only date guys you would marry because you can't help who you fall in love with. Keep your standards high. It may seem that no one is watching, but pray that you will be convicted. And remember that you will be accountable for your actions even if your best friend didn't know that anything happened. The greatest temptation is to spend *too* much time with anyone you are dating and lose sight of your standards. As my Mom always said, "Nothing good ever happens after midnight." What a challenge, because the "real" world lacks rules. You are the one to decide what they are.

—Age 28

Pray, Pray, Pray

I wish someone had told me to not have a serious boyfriend in college but just have a good time and date (innocently); I think it makes a difference for when you get married later on. I am happy I met other men in graduate school and waited until my late 20s to get married. I then felt that my husband was the best of the crop. Try to work and pursue a career early on, so that when you do get married or have children you won't look back and regret. You could stay home if you want and be content. The power of prayer is amazing. Before doing anything in your 20s, pray, pray, and pray about it. These will be decisions that could affect the rest of your life.

—Age 28

So what should I look for in a dating relationship? A Christian should look for another Christian—one who knows and seeks after God. If your guy can talk about everything under the sun except spiritual things . . . *be careful!* A person will soon talk about their feelings. If the man you are dating does not care about spiritual things now, while he is seeking to win your heart, he will not later on when he has won it!

"*D*o not be yoked together with unbelievers. For what do righteousness and wickedness have in common? Or what fellowship can light have with darkness? What harmony is there between Christ and Belial? What does a believer have in common with an unbeliever?"

—2 Corinthians 6:14–15

Never Settle

A couple of weeks ago, a stranger gave me a great piece of advice: "Never confuse loneliness for love." It is so true! Many of your friends will get married and you may feel left behind. Please don't. Enjoy this time of your life, as you will really get to know yourself. This is time that you will never be able to have back. Also, never settle for less or sell yourself short. I can tell you that I have had some dates/relationships that I really wanted to work and I just couldn't see what was missing. I was blinded. I finally figured out that often, God took the person out of my life because I couldn't. And stepping outside of the box now, I can see it.

—Age 26

Most people search and search for the right person when the key should be *being* the right person. Rather than spending our time looking, we ought to be working on becoming the right kind of person. And what qualities should we develop?

Be a woman who seeks after God. "Like a gold ring in a pig's snout is a beautiful woman who shows no discretion." (Proverbs 11:22).

Be a woman with a quiet and gentle spirit. "Your beauty should not come from outward adornment, such as braided hair and the wearing of gold jewelry and fine clothes. Instead, it should be that of your inner self, the unfading beauty of a gentle and quiet spirit, which is of great worth in God's sight." (1 Peter 3:3-4).

When I met my boyfriend, my life seemed so perfect that I quit depending on God for my daily bread. When that boyfriend broke up with me, I started to crumble. We were both Christians and our relationship had seemed to be glorifying to God.

However, I had not searched my heart and I did not realize that I was depending on my boyfriend for happiness and not on the Lord. I struggled for a year to finally discover that God is truly sufficient for all my needs! Even my needs of love, joy, and pleasure. I am a sanguine personality type, which means my goal is to have fun. I had to learn how to depend on God without having a boyfriend. I had a horrible summer at a wonderful camp because I still couldn't trust that God was all I needed. I was still concentrating on how to show my boyfriend there was not a reason for us to break up.

The Lord also brought me through that time, and taught me that all I need is Him, and now I am married to an amazing man. Our relationship is brilliant because we both depend on God for our needs. How special that time is now in my life, as it also reminds me of how wonderful my life really is, when it is in God's hands.

—Age 22

Not Sure What He Wants

Man-woman relationships should be approached with the utmost caution, and with standards set before the relationship starts, not while in the midst of it. I had a male friend, and we spent time together in various groups. We were not dating, but others began to speculate. My friends asked me if I liked him or could ever "see myself with him." I found myself secretly feeding those thoughts and beginning to have feelings for him. Everyone said he liked me, but he never pursued me.

We worked at the same camp that next summer, and it turned into the most painful experience I have ever been through. He kissed me (many times!) but never once pursued me or clearly stated where we stood in our relationship. This started an emotional roller coaster that still is causing me heartache. The last thing a girl needs is a guy who is "not sure what he wants." We need and deserve a strong, bold, confident man of God, one who is sure of his wants and convictions, and certain of what he believes. He knew that he liked me, but he wasn't completely sure. I bought into this for two and half years. As we became more and more physical, we remained "best friends," but this man saw no need to put the title of dating on our relationship. Soon my heart was entrenched in the situation. I truly believed that I was in love with him, and I had not guarded my heart, because I thought we were "just friends." I mean, who guards their heart in a friendship? Well, I should have. It was my responsibility to do so, not alone of course, but by the power of the Holy Spirit.

This story does not have a happy ending. I called it quits with this "friend" and have put the last three years behind me. I have suffered because I chose to allow this mixed relationship—it seemed the more "fun" option. If a guy ever reveals his feelings for you but does not follow up with action by pursuing you, that is a red flag to get out of that relationship. Thinking that he will change or mature is a waste of time and will only cause heartache. You may end up waiting for a long time and at the end have nothing to show for it.

—Age 23

A quick checklist for successful dating: Does the man love and seek God with his whole heart? Does he behave responsibly in the relationship and is he thoughtful? Are you a woman who loves and seeks God? Do you have a quiet and gentle spirit? Are you striving to be all God wants you to be?

God is very interested in each date—where you go and who you are with. Not only is He interested—He's there! And He alone knows what is the very best for you in the world of dating and marriage.

Marriage and Sex

So much of the emphasis in our society today has to do with sexuality, being sexy, and sexual drives. We live in a culture that has gone crazy over sex—advertisements, movies, songs, and television constantly portray sex as the way to utopia. When people turn away from God and the teachings of the Bible, one of the first places it shows is in the area of sexual things. It can be difficult to shape our thoughts about sex with so many opinions being thrown at us from all directions. The best thing to do is to look at God's Word to see what He has to say about sex.

We are God's creation, and sex is His creation. Nowhere does the Bible present sexuality, the sexual nature of man, or the sexual act as ugly or sinful in itself. On the contrary—it is one of God's wonders. Misused, it can be the devil's own tool, but isn't that true of any of God's best gifts? God has made us sexual beings. Sex as He intended it is not only good, but great! God alone understands our sexual nature with all its ramifications. He understands the pressures of today.

God is not outdated. If we accept the Bible as God's revealed thoughts and stake our future on what it says about Christ's deity, atonement, and resurrection, then it only stands to reason that what He says about sex is filled with real wisdom, love, and knowledge of those He has created.

How then does God view sex? "So God created man in his own image, in the image of God he created him; male and female he created them. God blessed them and said to them, 'Be fruitful and increase in number; fill the earth and subdue it. Rule over the fish of the sea and the birds of the air and over every living creature that moves on the ground.'...God saw all that he had made, and it was very good." (Genesis 1:27–28, 31). God's attitude toward sex is that it is very good.

> "*Haven't* you read,' he replied, 'that at the beginning the Creator "made them male and female," and said, "For this reason a man will leave his father and mother and be united to his wife, and the two will become one flesh"? So they are no longer two, but one. Therefore what God has joined together, let man not separate.'"
> —Matthew 19:4–6

God designed sex to be fun and intends for it only to be in the context of marriage. He intends for husbands and wives to be faithful to each other.

> "*May* your fountain be blessed, and may you rejoice in the wife of your youth. A loving doe, a graceful deer—may her breasts satisfy you always, may you ever be captivated by her love."
> —Proverbs 5:18–19

"*But* since there is so much immorality, each man should have his own wife, and each woman her own husband."

—1 Corinthians 7:2

The Bible tells us that God's desire is for individuals to have the most exciting sex life possible, but only within the confines and safety of marriage. He is in favor of sex within marriage but is flatly against it before and out of marriage.

"*It* is God's will that you should be sanctified: that you should avoid sexual immorality; that each of you should learn to control his own body in a way that is holy and honorable, not in passionate lust like the heathen, who do not know God."

—1 Thessalonians 4:3–5

As deep as the sexual drive is, it is not an isolated thing and cannot be separated from the total person. For the woman it is so intricately woven into her entire psyche that to separate it is to tear living fibers apart. Many who consider themselves liberated, modern, unshackled have time after time come crashing into the stark reality of the facts of their own nature. Sex with a man, with all its momentary ecstasy, is never enough. Women want to really belong to him and hunger for permanence. Sex outside of marriage goes against the way God made us, our whole being. For a while it may be exciting, but for most women a broken sexual relationship is sheer agony. Few women are able to easily face the idea of sharing their man with someone else—now, a year from now, or ever.

When God says, "two shall be one flesh," as old-fashioned and unpopular as this may sound in the twenty-first century, He is saying that something very real is happening. There has been a mingling of life itself. You are not the same as you were before being joined with that man. God intended this to be a permanent arrangement—not as something casual or just a physical release.

It is important to quickly state the fact that there is forgiveness with God. He is able to cleanse as we confess our failures to Him. But with forgiveness comes the realization of consequences and scars. God does not give us restrictions against sex in order to ruin our fun. On the contrary, He only wants to give us the very best!

A 24-year-old woman shares her thoughts.

The Most Precious Thing

Of course, I know that it is God's command and will for us to wait until we get married for sex. I think that this is the most precious thing that you could ever give your spouse. Can you think of anything more special or intimate or personal? Virginity is something that you have kept to yourself for a lifetime and that you can finally share with someone. I think that is what God wants for your life, and the way He designed things to be. Along the same lines, strive to make your relationships as pure as possible. It is so true that in being with someone physically you are bonding with them emotionally. Especially as a woman, this is dangerous.

—Age 24

Regrets

I want to say to girls who have compromised physically in a relationship, you can be forgiven. It took me a long time to realize that. If I had messed up so badly, how could anyone forgive me? First of all I had to come to realize that God had forgiven me, and then I had to forgive myself. This was the hardest for me to overcome. Satan definitely kept putting thoughts in my mind such as, 'You are worthless, no one will ever love you again because of the choices you made.' I began praying every day for God to take those thoughts away and for Him to help me to forgive myself, and over time that's exactly what happened. God has given me a second chance. He has given all of us second chances. The cool thing for me to see is that even though I messed up God still loves me and He has blessed me with a guy who still loves me too. That is unconditional love. So I will leave you with my favorite verse of all time: "'For I know the plans I have for you,' declares the LORD, 'plans to prosper you and not to harm you, plans to give you hope and a future'" (Jeremiah 29:11).

—Age 22

Love is not sex and sex is not love. God has designed sex as a physical expression between married people. Love is capable of growing without sex, but sex without love is extremely destructive.

The following are excerpts from a letter written by a 23-year-old woman to her fiancé. They had been dating for several years and it was becoming increasingly more difficult to stick to their standards. Instead of lowering the bar, they decided to raise it. In speaking with me, she wanted to make it clear that for them sex included all physical intimacy. In raising their standards, they chose to focus on how best to remain pure instead of how far is too far. The Bible was her authority as she wrote this heartfelt letter. But she quickly adds … this was the most difficult decision ever!

Sex in Marriage

1 Corinthians 6:18-20: "Flee from sexual immorality. All other sins a man commits are outside his body, but he who sins sexually sins against his own body. Do you not know that your body is a temple of the Holy Spirit, who is in you,

whom you have received from God? You are not your own; you were bought at a price. Therefore honor God with your body."

Sexual desires and activities must be placed under Christ's control. God created sex for procreation, pleasure, and as an expression of love and commitment between husband and wife. Sexual experience must be limited to the marriage relationship to avoid hurting ourselves, our relationship to God, and our relationship to others. God's rules are not to punish us, but to protect us and give us the fullest life in Him. If we focus on how much we can do without actually breaking the rules, we are defeating the purpose and missing out on the fullness God has to offer.

Romans 6:11–14 says, "In the same way, count yourselves dead to sin but alive to God in Christ Jesus. Therefore do not let sin reign in your mortal body so that you obey its evil desires. Do not offer the parts of your body to sin, as instruments of wickedness, but rather offer yourselves to God, as those who have been brought from death to life; and offer the parts of your body to him as instruments of righteousness. For sin shall not be your master, because you are not under law, but under grace."

Because of Jesus' ultimate sacrifice, we are no longer under the law, but under grace. We must live by the spirit of the law, not the letter of the law. So we should focus on the big picture of what pleases God instead of abusing the grace He gave us and focusing on what we can "get away with." Mental picture: God looking down from heaven and seeing an unmarried couple engaging in all sexual acts except penetration. What would God think? As 1 Corinthians says, "Everything is permissible, but not everything is beneficial." We should use our time, energy, and bodies as instruments of righteousness to bring glory to Him.

Any girl who says she can separate the physical from the emotional is lying to herself, or has been wounded before and became callous as a result. When you date different people, and share sexual experiences with them, you must become callous to sex to some degree in order to be able to break that "soul-tie" and move on to someone else. Sex becomes nothing but physical pleasure. This is probably why people often talk about their "first time" as being burned. They trusted too much. They could never imagine themselves with another person, because they are so in love and focused on the person they are with now. Then in subsequent relationships, they seem to be able to handle it better because they've learned not to let the physical aspect of the relationship mean too much. It's sad that people would have to separate the two and learn not to trust too much . . . when that is exactly what God meant for it to be . . . to enhance a marriage by strengthening trust, love, and commitment. God intended for us not to be able to separate the two, because then it is part (only one part) of the glue that bonds two hearts together.

As she draws her letter to its conclusion, she adds, "Now on the lighter side...I talked about the purpose for procreation, love, and commitment...but we must not forget God's purpose for it to be pleasure! As C.S. Lewis put it...'you can't take sex too seriously all the time.' I can't wait until we are married!"

God gives us commands about sex as a safeguard against damage that can be done when it is misused. Unfulfilled emotional needs often lead to frustration and bitterness and can become a crippling emotional habit—a way to try to fulfill the need for security and love. God wants to protect us for marriage—to protect our dignity. No other sin affects the body as sex does.

"Flee from sexual immorality. All other sins a man commits are outside his body, but he who sins sexually sins against his own body. Do you not know that your body is a temple of the Holy Spirit, who is in you, whom you have received from God? You are not your own; you were bought at a price. Therefore honor God with your body."

—1 Corinthians 6:18–20

And, for the Christian, every act of adultery or fornication excludes Christ. Is it worth it?

"No temptation has seized you except what is common to man. And God is faithful; he will not let you be tempted beyond what you can bear. But when you are tempted, he will also provide a way out so that you can stand up under it."

—1 Corinthians 10:13

Christians are tempted sexually just like everyone else. No one is exempt from temptation. As we confess our sin to God, He will forgive us. As we accept His forgiveness, we must also repent. Stop repeating sexual sins.

Marriage was designed by God and is very much on the minds of twentysomethings. He has a plan for each individual. How important it is to move with His plans and His timing. And to remember—no two relationships are alike.

Looking for the "Perfect Man"

One of the biggest fears I had about life after college was meeting someone to date and marry. Once you graduate everyone wants to know "who you are dating." These pressures can be especially forceful from family members. Once I was tired of looking for the "perfect man" and just enjoyed being where God had me at that very time in my life, I was content. I always kept wanting a companion. God wanted to meet those desires. I really just started having fun with our time together; then the Lord brought my husband into my life.

—Age 27

Marrying Your College Sweetheart

I met my husband during our freshman year of college. We dated continuously throughout our college years and then got married after graduation. I guess to other people we may have fit into the ongoing trend of marrying soon after college. To us, however, it was a different scenario. Not only were we in love; we knew that God wanted us to be married. After intense pre-engagement counseling, He sent the clear message. I did not marry my husband because it was the thing to do, because I was thrilled about having my dream wedding, or because I thought marriage would "complete" me. I married because this was God's plan.

—Age 26

The final thoughts come from a young woman who has seen marriage as a real adjustment to the "real" world.

Advice from a Young Married

Marriage may be years away for you, which is just fine, but if you're getting married soon, I have some words of wisdom for you from the real world. First of all, if, in the first few months of your marriage, you wake up in a cold sweat with your heart pounding and the certain knowledge that you've made the biggest mistake of your life, don't freak out. This is a perfectly normal reaction to the huge life transition that is marriage, and it isn't a sign you're headed straight for divorce court. My husband and I got married right after college and moved straight to a foreign country with dreadful weather, unfriendly natives, and few of the comforts of home. Somehow, I failed to connect these facts to recurring thoughts like, "I can't believe I have to spend the rest of my life with this man who goes to the bathroom with the door open and won't make the bed." Four years later we're just fine, and I think you'll be okay too.

Second, DON'T WORRY IF THERE AREN'T CONSTANT FIREWORKS IN THE BEDROOM. We've all been influenced by those movies and magazine articles featuring newlyweds who simply can't keep their hands off each other. You may have worked these issues out well before you get married, but my husband and I had both waited. I honestly thought something was wrong with me when I was able to think about something other than sex in the first few weeks of marriage. As far as my experience is concerned, those movie newlyweds are unreal. There's a lot more to early marriage than sex, and it may take a good long time (I'm talking as long as a year here) for you to be fully comfortable in this area. So just relax and have fun.

Finally, MAKE IT A PRIORITY TO FORM LASTING MEMORIES NOW. My husband and I were so poor when we were first married that we rode our bikes in the freezing snow to avoid the $30 charge for a monthly subway pass. I thought my mother was crazy when she suggested that we go for broke and take a long vacation about a year into our marriage. Somehow we scraped together enough for a two-week adventure in Europe. We can still laugh each other to tears reminiscing about that trip (and my husband's decision to learn to drive stick on the spot to avoid the extra charge for an automatic rental car). And I wouldn't admit to just anyone how many nights I pull out our pictures from that trip just to relive it. If you want my honest opinion, I would skip the honeymoon altogether (when you're too exhausted and shell-shocked to really enjoy it anyway) and take a vacation in a year or so. I realize that it may sound like a horrible letdown to go straight back to work after the wedding, but I can tell you that my Parisian honeymoon was a big bomb. However you choose to celebrate your new marriage, document it fully and take every opportunity to remember it with joy.

—Age 26

In the meantime, if you don't have a steady dating relationship and you are not headed to the altar—make the most of your friendships. Hopefully, you'll have only one husband, but life should be filled with many wonderful friendships.

Friendships

seven

Friendship is one of the greatest gifts that God has given us. In the transition from college to the real world, true, genuine, supportive friendships are of utmost importance. But friendships are hard work and take effort on both sides for a true friendship to be formed. This can be especially difficult in the real world, as there is no longer a real structure and consistency to facilitate meeting and making new friends.

Friends Outside Work

I encourage people to surround themselves with a support group of friends that can be trusted. Oftentimes, college graduates are forced to move away from friends, family, and support networks in order to obtain a position or start a career. I feel that it is very important when moving to an area with few friends or support networks to make it a priority to develop these things. This will make your transition and overall experience in the new area much smoother. I also feel that developing relationships outside of your job offers a more neutral atmosphere and relationship that can be more trusting, honest and open. Working as a young professional for three years now has opened my eyes to the politics of the 'real world' and the importance of watching what I say to whom and when I say it. A girl needs to have friends she can feel comfortable talking to about her feelings without having to fear that she is adversely affecting her career, endangering a promotion or respect from her coworkers just because her opinions, thoughts, or feelings differ from theirs.

—Age 25

Jesus said, "This is my commandment, that you love one another, just as I have loved you. Greater love has no one than this, that one lay down his life for his friends" (John 15:12-13). In the "real" world friendships can be a source of deep encouragement. Ecclesiastes 4:9-11 tells us, "Two can accomplish more than twice as much as one, for the results can be much better. If one falls, the other pulls him up; but if a man falls when he is alone, he is in trouble. Also, on a cold night, two under the same blanket gain warmth from each other, but how can one be warm alone?"

Christians and Non-Christians

Find good friends. Surround yourself with people who do not look at you like you are crazy when you say—"I will pray for you," or "Will you pray for me?" But at the same time, don't cut off people just because they are not Christians—your actions may change their mind and help them find Jesus. This is a hard task but one we are called to do as Christians!

—Age 26

A person's choice of close friendships speaks volumes about character. We will become like our closest friends. Surround yourself with people who are honest, strong in character, kind, wise, holy, and even thrifty. This can be difficult in the real world . . . especially in the workplace.

What We Need for Happiness

The things we feel sure we need for happiness can lead to our ruin. I learned this in the area of friendships. In college it seemed easy for me to gravitate toward Christian girls and invest in these friendships. Life after college is not that easy, especially if you decide to work in the real world. Friendships knitted together in Christ cannot be unwoven, but friendships of the world crumble and fall apart. Working as a schoolteacher has shocked me in many respects, especially in the teachers' lounge. In a place where you would think that love and purity of heart would reside, I found quite the opposite. Wanting to fit in my new working environment, I was tempted, and am tempted daily, to engage in unwholesome talk, gossip, and slander. God is quick to remind me that I am different, His child, and that I am called to be a light in the world, not a shadow in darkness. So what I thought would make me happy really darkened my heart. I know that this environment is not exclusive to schoolteachers. This can be applied to many aspects in life: relationships, money, material possessions; you fill in the blank. Just remember the Proverbs 31 woman and all that she stood for. Seek God in everything, and you will find Him everywhere!"

—Age 26

Friends can help with problems as well as be a sounding board. Friends help us to see our potential and we help them to see theirs.

The more whole and complete we are, the better friend we are. When I am secure and happy in myself I can better reach out to others, and reaching out is the name of the game in life beyond college graduation.

When We Are Ready

Another thing I've experienced is how once you are out of college, you are no longer in the same stage of life that you have been with your friends. Up until your post-college years, you are going through the same experiences as your friends. After college, so much change occurs that you may not be experiencing anything else that your best friend is experiencing. And you can't compare yourself to others in that respect. I believe that God prepares all of us for our futures individually, according to when we are ready. God knows what's best for you; you don't! But there is no reason to get down on your life according to what you have or have not experienced. Life is fragile and you only have one, so live it to your fullest, and everything else will fall into place accordingly.

—Age 25

Roommate Recommended

Find a roommate, or live near young people. I went to a small girls' school; there were a fewer than 200 girls in my graduating class, and we lived in dorms for four years. My friends were like sisters. This was an experience most people do not understand unless you have experienced single-sex education. When we graduated we went in different directions. That is when I realized the importance of a roommate. Roommates help you stay involved, and a roommate is another great way to meet tons of new people!

—Age 26

Roommate Difficulties

Roommates after college are unlike roommates in college, where most of the time you have similar schedules and social lives coincide. When you enter the "real world" things change significantly. Sometimes, if one roommate's job is more exciting than the other's, or one makes more money than the other, or perhaps you want to go out with your work friends and don't invite your roommate—and those situations start becoming difficult. Or even simple things like two totally different schedules can create a rift in the roommate situation.

—Age 24

Strengthened Values

Challenging myself intellectually and meeting new and different people helped strengthen my values and convictions. Although I was living in a southern city, most of the people in my law school class came from the northeast or west. I learned so much from them—just by dropping preconceived notions and allowing my heart to see people. I may not have approved of their lifestyle or agreed with their views and choices, but those differences only made me a stronger person. For the first time in my life, people challenged my views and forced me to look inside and try to vocalize why I believe what I do.

—Age 26

Out of the Bubble

Be open-minded: I thought that I was Miss Independent in college, but now looking back I was living in a world of people exactly like me. Wealthy and WASP-y was my world. I love my friends, and it's a gift to surround yourself with

Christian friends. I have heard a lot of people say that befriending non-Christians puts you in a "lukewarm," "fence riding" position. I think that it's crucial to have your Christian friends as support, but relationships are not an either-or situation. I've learned more about why I believe what I believe, and where I stand from my non-Christian friends. Challenge yourself to get out of your comfort zone, and by the way, variety is the spice of life. Living in a bubble essentially denies yourself of a richer spiritual life.

—Age 24

Life After College?

Living in Los Angeles, California, I am surrounded with the most fascinating, interesting, intelligent people, yet people with no morals. Apathy sets in as I realize that I do not know one single attractive Christian male. What does this mean? A year ago, I thought that life, in a way, would be over at graduation; that, after college, all I had left to do was settle down. All the fun and excitement would be over. I realize now how much I have to learn, how much I have to do. The possibilities that once seemed few are now endless. Life has just begun. Certainly, there is life after college that outweighs even those "best years of your life."

—Age 22

Singles Classes

I remember in college vowing that I would never go to a singles class. I just made a judgmental blanket statement that all singles classes were simply "meat markets" and I did not want any part in that. After I was back home, I slowly warmed up to the fact that "single" was my phase in life and I would much rather meet friends at church than at a bar, so it only made sense to go. God used that time in my life to bless me with several close friendships and many fun memories. I guess when you graduate, one of the big culture shocks is that suddenly all of your close friendships are gone and you are forced to start all over again. This can result in some lonely times as you try to build new friendships. But I learned that I just had to place myself in situations with people that I knew would be quality people with similar beliefs and standards as myself. And the easiest way to find such a group to get plugged in with, for me, was through the singles group at church. I think I also expected it to be almost like when you pledge a sorority, in that you come in and you are instant friends because none of you really have anyone else. But it really wasn't like that at all. I found that I really had to make more of an effort to make friends. People are busy with work and other things, so friendships just don't come as easily as they do in college when you have so much free time. But singles groups really do provide opportunities to make the transition to new friendships easier.

—Age 26

The Comparison Game

One of the most important things I am convicted of is the destructive nature of comparison. As graduation threw my friends and me onto different paths and into different seasons of life, I lost the false security that came with similarity. As I encountered the unexpected struggles of this new phase, I started depending less and less on times of solitude with the Lord. I was overwhelmed by the temptation to look to someone else who appeared to have it all together and to covet their position.

—Age 23

Spiritual Comparison

For some reason, I feel like I need to advise girls against comparisons. Perhaps it is because I have struggled so much with comparing myself to others. I think that this is so common and yet can destroy a person. There is rarely anything good that comes out of comparison. You either will walk away feeling better about yourself (pride) or you will feel worse about yourself (discouragement). Neither of these are of the Lord. The point that I finally got to was, why compare yourself with other people? You are unique, and God has specially designed and formed you. I am not saying be lazy and be complacent and don't strive for God's future for you. But do not get hung up on looking around and comparing yourself to other people. God is the one you should be comparing yourself to. Be sure that you are living up to His standards (whatever they are) for your life. It is not up to the people around you. And this applies especially to spiritual comparison. It is so hard not to spiritually compare yourself to those around you. God has equipped us all differently and we all have different spiritual gifts. That is why as we walk according to the light and do our "role" in the body, God will work through us and comparison is no longer relevant! Be free to be who you are!

—Age 24

After Graduation

As I reflect on my graduation, I remember feelings of excitement and anticipation as I left the college I called home for four years and prepared to face my future. After months of worrying about where I would go, I ended up moving home because I had been accepted into an internship and graduate school in my hometown. I felt fortunate because I didn't have to worry about a job or a place to live. I know that God had a hand in this as always, and I was extremely grateful because for the first time I felt peace about where I was going. However, I just knew I would never be able to find Christian friends like I was able to in high school and college. But once again, God's grace prevailed. I feel that one of the most important aspects of my life has been the relationships that I developed after college.

—Age 25

Keeping Up with College Friends

Some of your most precious and lifetime friends come from your college days. While I was still in school, an older and wiser friend of mine told me how blessed I was to have such strong and incredible friendships during college. He also said that I would have to work at maintaining those friendships and that our group would have to make efforts to get together consistently. At the time I thought there was no way we would have difficulty keeping up, getting together, and knowing what was going on with each other's lives. My friend was right—after a few years it takes effort, and at times it is hard, but it is so worthwhile. There is increasingly less time, I realize, to make new friends—especially those with whom you share so much in common. I encourage you (besides phone calls, emails, letters, and visits) to set aside a weekend every year with your closest friends—even if you live in the same town now. Go away for a weekend, take a trip, and just be with each other. If you wait until later, it will become more and more difficult—as friends get married, move away, have children, and begin new careers. These friends are a gift—allow them to continue to grow!

—Age 29

Bonded Forever

No one ever talks about the difficulties of the post-college years and your 20s. These years are trying times: some friends get married, some are single, some start having babies, some live in the hometown where we all grew up, and others are scattered across the United States. A true sense of "growing up" and the reality of the changes impacting our lives starts to hit home.

At least for me, this was the time that my relationship with God became the most important and most real. I found that I was no longer living in my "protective bubble." This was actually good for me because I was forced to seek God for myself and in my own way. However, I know the reason I was able to strengthen my relationship with God is because of the foundation that was built in me through Bible studies and discipleship groups.

While our friends do lead scattered lives now and have forged many different paths, there are still a handful of friends with whom I will be bonded forever, through the Lord. In times of both joy and sorrow, these friends and I can immediately put God in the center of our discussions. This is something for which I am eternally grateful.

—Age 26

It's important to love our friends and to be committed to them. But we need to be dependent on God, because He's the only One who will never leave us and He alone is able to meet our deepest needs and be our most intimate friend.

You can trust God with your life!

eight

Trusting God with Your Life

"Instead of facing the world head-on, recent grads hesitate to step out. They choose to wallow in the feel-good memories of academia. It's a critical time recent college grads face because they have to make decisions that could determine success, relationships and economic stability. A bad job market makes it harder. . . . The crisis for young adults has been steadily bubbling for the past five years. It's hit a boiling point because people are being laid off. There is little stability in most people's lives. That instability creates a lot of anxiety, and along with anxiety comes feelings of helplessness. Quarter-lifers blame the economy, a changed job landscape and a huge array of options that fuel their self-doubt. There's a road map when you are in school. If you do a certain amount of work, you get a certain amount of credits and you graduate. It's a game...but then, all of a sudden, there is no road map that guarantees you where you want to go."

—*Denver Post*, January 6, 2003

"Therefore I tell you, do not worry about your life, what you will eat or drink; or about your body, what you will wear. Is not life more important than food, and the body more important than clothes? Look at the birds of the air; they do not sow or reap or store away in barns, and yet your heavenly Father feeds them. Are you not much more valuable than they? Who of you by worrying can add a single hour to his life?"

—Matthew 6:25–27

Life offers many things, many obstacles, many situations that are hard to understand and way out of our control. The transition to the "real" world paints numerous pictures of these very facts. Welcome to the world of instability! Actually, life is always unstable, but situations such as college life give us the illusion of control. So what do we do? How can we avoid the downward spiral of anxiety that leads to a feeling of helplessness?

We are not given the choice of being completely in control. There will be problems and plenty of them, to be sure, but we do have a choice as to how we will react to these problems. The best choice is the follow the teachings of Jesus where He tells us DO NOT WORRY! In the Sermon on the Mount, He tells us in detail about how to combat worry. Jesus also shows us what not to worry about. Don't worry about your life, what you eat and drink, what you wear. These are very basic needs in life. God wants us to give Him our needs, our wants, our desires. Let Him decide the direction of your life.

Advice for Planners

When I think back to when I was in college, there is only one thing I wish. I wish I had not spent so much time planning out my life, when I now realize that my life is not in my own hands. The Lord is in control and I know now that I have to relinquish the planning to Him and trust in the fact that things will work out according to His plan.

I have always been a planner. I am one of those people who keeps my calendar close at hand to write down important dates, events, and the infamous lists! When I was in college, I had my whole future before me and lots of ways to plan out my life. In the back of my mind (and I'm sure other planners are like this, too) I had a picture of the way I wanted things to work. I knew where I wanted to end up, the type of job I wanted to have, exactly when I would get married, have children, buy a home, etc. Yet the situation and circumstances changed. I have come to many forks in the road that involve major life decisions.

During one of these life-decision-making processes, I received the most important advice I have ever received. As I was agonizing over which road to take, my father came to me and said, "Pray. Pray as hard as you can. Then, listen to that voice inside of you. That voice is God." So, I took my dad's advice and prayed. When I was finished praying, I listened to that voice inside of me, and it felt like it was yelling! Now, when I have to make any decision, I pray. I try to hand over even the most miniscule things to the Lord, because I know He knows what is right for me.

Two of the most unexpected and unplanned circumstances in my life now are my wonderful husband and beautiful daughter. I found myself falling in love, getting married, and becoming a mother much earlier than I had planned. I have found that even though my life now is not exactly what I had pictured a few years ago, it is exactly what I want for myself at this moment. Sometimes the most wonderful blessings in life are the ones that are most unexpected.

—Age 25

A key to not worrying is found in this verse: "But seek first his king-dom and his righteousness, and all these things will be given to you as well. Therefore do not worry about tomorrow, for tomorrow will worry about itself. Each day has enough trouble of its own." (Matthew 6:33–34).

There are many passages in the Bible that tell us not to worry. For instance: "Do not be anxious about anything, but in everything, by prayer and petition, with thanksgiving, present your requests to God" (Philippians 4:6). At times that is so difficult to do! Our human nature screams at us to worry, but God says don't. Instead, pray.

Pray, Pray, Pray

The first advice I would give to girls preparing for life after college is pray, pray, pray! I worried so much about what to do with my life post-graduation. I always had worries and thoughts running in the back of my mind as senior year progressed. I could see time slipping by and still I didn't know what I would do or where I would go. I finally made myself turn those worries into prayers. I set a routine, weekly time to pray specifically about my direction after college. I took an hour-long window of time every Wednes-day (during which I usually had lunch) and spent that time in my little study carrel in the library fasting, praying, read-ing my Bible, and journaling. As I prayed, I would write down verses that God showed me and I'd also meditate about where I saw myself and where I wanted to go. Gradu-ally, God helped me narrow down in my mind three cities where I thought I'd like to move. I prayed about those and they gradually narrowed down to 1 city (Washington, D.C.). That process continued in all aspects of my life after col-lege—housing, roommates, job, etc. Always, it just took really pressing in with prayer and looking to God, trusting in His promises for provision and guidance, and in time He leveled the mountains. He was leveling them all along.

Having that time to really focus and release my worries to God and to sort through my ideas made such a difference. It not only helped me find guidance, but helped free me from worrying about it during the rest of the week because I knew I was doing something about it on a regular basis.

—Age 24

God invites us to bring all our petitions and requests before Him. "Cast all your anxiety on him because he cares for you" (1 Peter 5:7). He desires for His children to look to Him in all situations, and that includes the potential anxiety that can creep in during your twenties.

Don't Be Afraid to Ask

Prayer is so important and it is crucial to our lives—allowing God to work in and through us. The Bible says that we don't have because we don't ask! That is huge! I ask God about anything and everything. I know that there are a lot of people who disagree with the fact that God cares about everything in our lives and every single detail. I disagree. I may be wrong but I know that my earthly father cares about all of my needs and concerns and questions, so how much more does God care, who made and created me? I would challenge you to pray for yourself and pray God's promises over yourself. Pray for peace and prosperity and good health. These are not selfish things to pray. Again, we do not have, because we do not ask! You may be the only person praying for you. That is okay and God longs to hear our needs. Pray for others, too, for sure! But don't be scared in praying protection, God's will, and blessing in your life. I believe that He loves hearing from

His children. He knows our needs before we know them, but He loves for us to come to Him and to trust Him and to ask Him for every desire of our heart! God has better plans for you than you could ever have for yourself.

—Age 24

Often God allows situations to come into our lives that may tempt us to worry. These very situations develop staying power so that we may learn how to trust in and rely upon God in even greater ways. Remember to "Consider it pure joy, my brothers, whenever you face trials of many kinds, because you know that the testing of your faith develops perseverance. Perseverance must finish its work so that you may be mature and complete, not lacking anything" (James 1:2-4). Hard times give us endurance and this produces perfection and completeness.

Hold on to God

My life has faced many changes since those fun, carefree days of college, almost five years ago. Most people thought my story was the perfect script, but I was just beginning a new chapter—a long, hard journey with the Lord. I graduated in May, married my college sweetheart in June, moved to a new state in July, and buried my dearest friend in the world, my mom, in August. I had to pick up the pieces of my life, go back to my new home, find a job, and put my new husband through graduate school. Most people do not undergo that much change and stress all at once, but leaving college and entering "the real world" is not an easy transition.

Most seasons of our lives as girls seem to involve some type of identity crisis. From trends and fashion wars with our girlfriends in grade school, to the confusing temptations and desperate longings to be liked in high school, and then college and facing the same question again, "Who am I?" I asked myself that question again today. God designed us as women to need to know the answer. Who am I? Does anyone know I exist? Do they care? Do they love me? And no matter what your answer: a great job, a gorgeous husband, a wonderful Bible study, a cute new home, a precious baby . . . nothing will ever satisfy those questions but Jesus.

I belong to God. I am His through Jesus. And I will never be the same.

Now that may sound overly simplistic to you. But as we all ask the hard questions about life and God, nothing solidifies that answer more than walking through suffering with Him. From my brokenness, my loss, and my cries from the depths of my heart, God has met me on the other side to help me say, "Yes, I do believe. God does exist. He does love me, and I can trust Him." If you can hold onto God, you will be a woman with a genuine heart, a deep soul, and a passionate faith.

—Age 27

Anytime a trial comes into our life it is meant for our good—to make us a person who is able to trust God in a deeper way. A very real trial is change—where things do not go as we planned. But we can remember to "give thanks in all circumstances, for this is God's will for you in Christ Jesus" (1 Thessalonians 5:18). The most wonderful fact is the certainty that in an ever-changing world, God will never change.

I Want the World to Stop

The only thing that has been a constant in my life since graduation is change. Thankfully, even my relationship with God has been changing. These days I am learning to rely heavily on

His constancy and unfailing love because so much around me seems uncertain. With graduations, marriages, new jobs, graduate school, and babies, every day seems to bring with it more goodbyes and hellos than a heart can bear. Some days it seems like everyone is moving on with their lives except me. Sometimes I want the world to stop for a minute so I can catch up. Some days my honest prayer is, God, where are You? Do You remember me? Where are You at work in my life? But day by day I am learning that God is always right here with me, fully knowing me—He is the same yesterday, today, and forever. God is faithful. I often remember 2 Timothy 2:13, "if we are faithless, he will remain faithful, for he cannot disown himself." Praise God that His faithfulness is not dependent on our faith. All around me situations and relationships may be changing, but His love endures forever.

—Age 24

"Trust in the LORD and do good; dwell in the land and enjoy safe pasture. Delight yourself in the LORD and he will give you the desires of your heart. Commit your way to the LORD ; trust in him and he will do this" (Psalm 37:3–5). Life does change and there are many different seasons of life. And God can be trusted with those seasons both good and difficult.

Seasons of Life

A big lesson I have learned during this time is about seasons of life. People, boyfriends, roommates, jobs, and family are all seasonal. I have learned the seasons do change. During this time I have married off many friends, changed jobs, lost my mother, changed boyfriends, and bought a house! I had to realize that my security does not lie in these things but in Christ. In this Christian life we will suffer and I can say that through my suffering these past three years, I have grown in my faith. Overall, my advice is to enjoy this time, but use it to completely grow in Christ. Without your faith grounded you are bound to let seasonal changes and suffering really affect you.

—Age 26

I think the greatest thing that we can do as young adults with our lives is trust God with our whole heart. He is so moved by our desire to wait on Him and press into Him. God never disappoints us and He always has our best interest in mind. It is hard for me to understand this and to accept God's goodness and fullness in our lives. It is the old mindset that God is a skimpy God who only wants us to have enough to get us by. However, God wants us to have His very best. But He has to work out His plan and purposes in our lives first. He has to instill in us His character and integrity before He can trust us with His most precious possessions.

—Age 24

Be careful if you move home because home isn't as you knew it anymore.

—Age 24

The key to surrender is trust. We'll never be able to fully trust someone without having a relationship with that person. The same is true of God. The deeper our intimacy with Him, the more we're able to let go and let Him direct our lives.

Relationship with God

God reveals Himself. He desires a relationship. He wants His children to seek after Him—to run toward Him. Jesus wants to be our first priority. "But *seek first* his kingdom and his righteousness, and all these things will be given to you as well" (Matthew 6:33). God's kingdom and God's righteousness should be the ultimate goal for our lives—even in the "real" world. This determines where I work, with whom I spend my time, whom I marry, what I do with my money, and how I spend my time. Choosing one thing over all the rest for the rest of life is a difficult thing to do. But Jesus says in effect, "This is your priority; this comes first." And as we place Him in His rightful position, our lives are joyful, productive, and fulfilled.

Spending Time with God

No matter what you are doing, always make time for the Lord. Around November of my first year of teaching, there was a day in which we did not have to be at school until

11:00, and I had time for a morning devotion. I had my devotion that morning and haven't stopped since. It has been so sweet just to sit in the presence of our sovereign Lord before I start my day. Now that I am in the habit, I cannot imagine starting it any other way! The early morning hours may take a while to get used to, but it is well worth it when your relationship with Christ begins to grow. For me, mornings are the best time. If you are a night owl, then so be it. Just don't let anything get in the way of your time with God.

The Lord has continued to show me Scripture that demonstrates the importance of just sitting in His presence. More than our acts of service, He desires us! "You do not delight in sacrifice, or I would bring it; you do not take pleasure in burnt offerings. The sacrifices of God are a broken spirit; a broken and contrite heart, O God, you will not despise" (Psalm 51:16–17). He wants our hearts. He wants us to be completely and totally in love with Him. But we won't fall in love with Him until we get to know Him. And we can't get to know Him if we don't spend time with Him.

I love the story of Mary and Martha in Luke 10:38–42. Jesus much more preferred Mary sitting at His feet and worshipping Him than Martha's service to Him. Sometimes we can get so caught up in serving God that we forget to just rest in His presence in worship and adoration. Spend time with the Lord. Instead of trying to squeeze Him into your busy schedule, spend time with Him first and then squeeze in the rest!

—Age 25

First in My Life

Life can be filled with so many things, so much busyness. It is my prayer daily that Christ will be first in my life and that I will hunger to know Him first. To me that even means making Him the first Person I meet with each day, and the first One I learn from and listen to. When I seek Him first, my life seems more balanced and I have peace despite my circumstances.

—Age 23

One of the most important things we can do as Christians is to take time daily to read God's Word and meditate upon it. As we do, we will grow to know Him better and love Him more. By living according to God's Word we're able to live a pure life. It is God's Word in the heart that keeps us from sin. God's Word is meant to teach, rebuke, correct, and train in righteousness. It helps us live the Christian life.

Develop a Relationship

Develop a relationship with God. Spend time with Him and study His Word. Learn to trust Him fully and let Him have complete control of your life even though sometimes that is hard to do. Be courageous and step out of the boat when He calls you to do so. You'll be blessed in ways you can't imagine. Journal. You'll be able to look back and see where God has worked in your life.

—Age 22

"Blessed is the man who does not walk in the counsel of the wicked or stand in the way of sinners or sit in the seat of mockers. But his delight is in the law of the LORD, and on his law he meditates day and night. He is like a tree planted by streams of water, which yields its fruit in season and whose leaf does not wither. Whatever he does prospers" (Psalm 1:1-3). Our attitude toward God's Word should be one of delight as we meditate upon it. And as we do this, our lives will be stable and prosperous.

Most Important Time of Your Life

I believe this is probably the most important time of your life. It's a time of searching for love, significance, and a path of acceptance. You're at a crossroads—no one is holding your hand any longer. It's all you—and what an exciting opportunity sits before you. An adventure—along with the insecurities and fear—an adventure that will lead you along a new path. None of us know what this path will look like, or is even supposed to look like—all we know is to close our eyes and walk. This is the first time in your life when you'll truly have the opportunity to walk by faith—to hold onto the core values of Jesus Christ and to learn what this life is really all about. You're going to have the opportunity to draw closer to Christ or further away. Yes, you may make it if you decide to go out on your own without Jesus, but I can promise this—it won't be pretty. It won't be fulfilling—it won't be purposeful—and you won't find what you truly want. What do you want? Let me save you the time and money from hours of counseling . . . joy. It only comes from one place. Knowing Him.

—Age 24

Look Vertically

Try to keep your eyes looking up, vertically, at God, rather than looking horizontally at your circumstances. As you job search, and make that transition out from under your parents financially, and as you begin to separate from college friends and make new friends, trials and tribulations and lonely times can certainly creep in. Don't get down and turn to things of this world to numb the pain—for example: alcohol, compulsive shopping, overexercising, overeating, or undereating. Turn to God. He cares! Spend time with our Lord. He knows what you are feeling; tell Him everything.

—Age 26

God Used Every Step

My three years out of college have taught me a lot. I have become a new person—grown to fully love and understand myself. I didn't take the easy route—I moved to a city where I knew no one, lived alone, and went to law school where I was unsure of my abilities—and God used every step to teach me and show me His plan for my life. I can't say that I was happy with Him all the time, but my life is a testament to how following Him can make you the happiest you will ever be.

—Age 26

Everyone Has Worries

Everyone has similar worries after college: careers, finances, living arrangements, friendships, and relationships. I think that even the most prepared person will have unexpected challenges to face. That is truly what strengthens your relationship with God, the God you can always trust and love. I am only 25 years old, and I still don't know exactly what the next part of God's plan will hold, but I can trust that as He is protecting and loving me, I can face the future with a smile and a forever friend in the Lord.

—Age 25

The most important way that God's Word renews life: it shows a person how they can have eternal life, become part of Christ's family. The Bible is the roadmap to heaven as well as a guide throughout life. "The law of the LORD is perfect, reviving the soul.

The statutes of the LORD are trustworthy, making wise the simple. The precepts of the LORD are right, giving joy to the heart. The commands of the LORD are radiant, giving light to the eyes" (Psalm 19:7–8).

Listening to God

I am a true believer that the family and friends you make along the way shape your life. While in college I was blessed with a wonderful circle of friends but I was very busy studying because I had the dream of going to medical school. When I realized that my life was consumed with studying, I knew I was not listening to what God wanted me to do with my life. After changing my major, I was able to focus on other important aspects of life; friends, socials, Bible study, and most importantly the Lord. I feel that reaffirming my faith has helped me to embark on life after college.

—Age 25

Stripped and Stretched

College was such a growing up time for me. As I was learning to live independently, dependent on God, I began to grow more intimate with the Lord. But it wasn't until I left my safe, secure "bubble" of the university that I have been stripped and stretched in ways that have given me a clearer understanding of who God is and who I am.

The stripping I've experienced in the real world has been painful but fruitful, and I want to share with you some examples of how these stripping times have actually become blessings. First, I have been stripped of the flexibility I loved at college. For instance, I used to be able to wake up late, go to class, head to a park for an hour-long quiet time with God, grab ice cream with a friend, and so on. Now, I have to go to

WORK. Therefore, my time with the Lord has been less in quantity. This limitation of my time, however, has shown me that God cares more about quality time than quantity, and that He longs for me to commune with Him throughout the entire day rather than just in my set-aside time. As I have been in the working world, I've really had to pray for the Lord to help me "practice His presence" in the mundane activities of everyday life. I have also come to realize that a quiet time doesn't equal a blessed day, and missing a quiet time doesn't yield a bad day. My legalistic views have been shattered quite a bit.

As I left college, I had an identity crisis. I was no longer in my familiar college circle, and I quickly realized that a lot of my security had come from knowing people and being known. Thankfully, God has been stripping this false security and pride, but it sure does hurt. I imagine you too will experience a similar identity stripping, but I challenge you to embrace this time and pray that the Father will make you so wrapped up in being His treasured daughter that you will rest secure in that identity alone.

I have also been stripped of some of my dreams since leaving college. I always dreamed of moving back home to the wonderful community where I grew up. I would picture myself strolling my babies with my best friend and her children. However, God knows best! It seems that He might be leading my husband and me overseas to the mission field—a little different than I had imagined. But I am learning to let God mold my dreams and paths because He is good and "loving toward all He has made."

—Age 25

Faith Must Be Sound

In the real world it is hard to find a Christian bubble. The real world is a motley crew of people from various religious backgrounds, which is much different from surrounding yourself with your fellow sorority sisters. I found this fun, exciting, and challenging. I learned quickly that my faith had to be sound! I needed to be able to defend my own beliefs in a loving way. The mission field in the real world is enormous, but scary, because you realize you are concerned about your coworkers' eternity—and you also realize that you will have to work with them the next day following any religious discussions. I remember how red my face got discussing salvation with my boss who thought everyone went to heaven. In the real world, you might find yourself as the one lone Christian in the workplace. Therefore, you must be prepared to have your walk rock solid personally and not identified with your group of friends.

—Age 28

Withdrawing from God

For awhile, I had no desire to be close to God. I'm not sure why I withdrew from Him during this time. I just know that I wanted to start enjoying life and catching up on all I had missed out on over the first 22 years of my life. This led to an indifferent attitude, which was totally unlike me. I was so unmotivated about everything. (The first year of your career is not the most opportune time to lose your motivation.) My close friends didn't know what to think. My personality had changed, and I was a different person. They didn't know what to do with someone who was so pessimistic all the time. One of them even suggested therapy or anti-depressants, both of which I refused. I hoped it was a phase that would eventually end.

However, toward the end of the year, I realized that I wasn't where I needed to be spiritually. I wasn't as close to God as I had been in high school and college. Then I had been surrounded by youth group friends or the wonderful friends I met through a Christian group on campus. I still had my college friends, but my daily work environment did not have a strong Christian support group. I continued to visit churches with serious thoughts of joining the one I attended the most, but I just couldn't do it. So there I was, knowing I wasn't where I should be spiritually, but with no desire to get back there. One day on the way to work I heard the FFH song "Lord Move, or Move Me." I said, "Lord, seriously, move me, push me, shove me, whatever You have to do. Just get me there!" Things really seemed to start turning around at my 23rd birthday. New Year's wasn't depressing for me. I think it was because I didn't have any expectations for the upcoming year like I had the previous year. I told a friend that I was no longer making plans for life and was leaving it up to God.

—Age 23

Jesus has been described as the "hound of heaven." He is forever looking after, running after, and running toward His children. He is a God of forgiveness and total redemption.

Mistakes and Redemption

ten

A fact of the real world is the total assurance that you will make mistakes and there will be trials. The Bible tells us this: "Dear friends, do not be surprised at the painful trial you are suffering, as though something strange were happening to you" (1 Peter 4:12). Problems arise from forces outside ourselves that deeply affect our lives and often find us powerless to change the situation. These trials show us our true selves. How do we react? How well do we stand?

We can look at it as an opportunity, a challenge, even a reason for rejoicing. "Consider it pure joy, my brothers, whenever you face trials of many kinds, because you know that the testing of your faith develops perseverance. Perseverance must finish its work so that you may be mature and complete, not lacking anything" (James 1:2–4).

God wants to know that we will trust Him even when it looks as if the whole world is crumbling down around us, spinning out of control, and totally unfair and unexplainable. It's one thing to say we love Jesus and believe in God when our lives are going well. But it is a totally different scenario when we are surrounded by trials. Hard times produce a faith that endures. We are asked to respond with joy because it gives God the freedom to work in the midst of that trial for our good and His glory. And He will. "And we know that in all things God works for the good of those who love him, who have been called according to his purpose" (Romans 8:28).

God knows what He is doing. He is totally sovereign, which means that no matter how bad a situation seems, God still has a redemptive plan that can only be realized through total surrender to His hand. We may not understand what is happening, but even in our confusion, God invites us to call upon Him for wisdom—for the ability to see life and all its problems from His perspective. "If any of you lacks wisdom, he should ask God, who gives generously to all without finding fault, and it will be given to him" (James 1:5).

Problems may be out of our control. We do not always have the power to change the situation. What we do have is the power to control our responses to those negative circumstances. The real world is full of real problems—financial, social, physical, and so on. Jesus is the real answer to all the questions.

A Story of Struggle

Struggle produces strength! Heartache and tribulations are often blessings in disguise leading us to a state of brokenness and powerlessness so that we can surrender ourselves and submit to God. This is a truly liberating and freeing experience, knowing that the creator of all things loves you as you are. He desires to heal our wounds, our hurts, and our hearts. Why does my past look the way it does? Am I to be ashamed?

A small list of struggles I have experienced includes:

- Insecurities (as a young Christian, as a woman, as a student, you name it—just being me!)
- Abandoning and walking away from Christ
- The aggravated sexual assault and rape of myself and two best friends after a typical weekend college party
- Having to testify in court years later against one of the four assailants, and witnessing him being sentenced to life in prison
- Rather than looking to God for direction as to how to deal with overwhelming emotions, turning to an eating disorder (bulimia) and alcohol as a source of comfort and coping mechanism
- Three years after graduating from college—meeting an incredible man, falling in love, getting engaged, taking part in an impure relationship, then calling off the engagement
- Admitting that my addictions not only dealt with food and bulimia, but grasping the fact of being an alcoholic (difficult concept being 25 years of age, fairly recently out of college)

How could I have turned out so WRONG? I realized I was:

- Ashamed of the rape (afraid of physical intimacy), ashamed of the alcoholism (lying and sneaking alcohol, carelessly endangering the lives of others)
- Ashamed of bulimia (binging on food to mask emotions I did not understand/know how to deal with, then throwing up the food in order to stay attractive)
- Ashamed of being too self-absorbed to care about others
- Ashamed of ending a relationship that felt so good (but learning that without taking care of myself, I will never be able to offer an honest and healthy love to anyone else)

None of the sins of my past, or sins yet to come have the power to entangle me, or separate me from the perfect love of Christ. He is the only man that will never fail me. Because of Jesus, and the grace He has shown me, tomorrow, February 5, 2003, I will be getting a purple coin ("chip") representing 9 months of continuous sobriety. I have truly had a spiritual awakening and know that I am not created for this world, but for eternity. My purpose on this earth is to love the Lord God with all my heart, love others (as selfishly as I have loved myself), and share the experience, strength, and hope Jesus Christ has given me at the expense of His life. It's all about GRACE, and once you've personally experienced His grace, you get a glimpse of His all-encompassing, redeeming, and healing love!

—Age 25

Forgiving Abuse

I had become a master at hiding my feelings. I appeared to be happy; even my own family did not realize how badly I was hurting inside. The real world is filled with people who are hurting so deeply and the tragedy is that no one knows how badly.

A counselor once told me that at the age of thirteen I had been through more than most forty-year-old women ever go through. By the time I was a young teenager I had been molested by three people who were very close to me— my grandpa, my brother, and a close family friend.

Death was something I learned about at a young age, growing up in a neighborhood full of violence. I couldn't walk out my front door without hearing some sort of shots being fired. I witnessed the death of a friend who was killed in a drive-by shooting. I have been to so many funerals—too many to even count—most being of friends who died because they were in a gang or just in the wrong place at the wrong time. My cousin was shot and killed when I was ten years old. I totally fell apart. Taking a major overdose of pills, I went to sleep, hoping to never wake again. Maybe I was just tired of dealing with the pain of seeing death all around me. God had a better plan for me as I woke up the next day and told no one of my suicide attempt.

At the age of fifteen, I awoke to my sister's screams. My dad was having a serious asthma attack. As I ran into the living room, I heard a gurgling sound. "God, help him," I prayed. I then said something I will never forget saying—"Dad, I love you." That was the first and last time. My dad stopped breathing and died in front of me. Pain has been my steady companion all through my life.

When I was 21 Jesus came to me and brought me inner healing. I walked into the counselor's room and three and half hours later, I walked out of that room a different person. Jesus met me at the points in my childhood where I had been abused and afraid. His nail-scarred hands took the little girl in His arms. As He led me through door after door of my heart, I realized that I must forgive each man who had abused me. I must know for certain that the abuse was not my fault. I could not say "I forgive" only in my mind. I must speak the words aloud. As I obeyed, my heart was released and for the first time I felt God's love.

Before that counseling session, I thought that God didn't love or care about me. God, however, showed me that His love is amazing. Nothing I have done or ever will do can change that love.

I still have a long way to go. There are still many things that God wants me to deal with, but I am confident that God is going to finish what He started in my life. Jesus came in and showed me all that I needed to see. I hope people will be encouraged by my testimony. For those who feel there is no hope, God loves you and He cares. There will always be a way. I am so glad that I allowed God to do some work in my life, and I pray that He will continue to do so. I desire to be all I was created to be and want to be ready to do what God has called me to do. The healed me is finally free!

—Age 22

Both of these young women have sought and found freedom. The cost has been great. But because they were able, by God's grace, to forgive those who had sinned against them, the damage was lessened. Had they chosen not to forgive, the cost would have been much greater.

But what about forgiving ourselves for what we have done? We will reap what we sow. There is no discouragement like the discouragement that comes from our own wrongdoing. Enduring the consequence of our own sin creates feelings of discouragement and grief that are difficult to describe. But once again, God is the answer and His grace is greater than anything we've done.

Once a person becomes a Christian, she does not have to give in to sin. Christ will always find a way of escape for us if we will let Him do so. However, because we want our own way, we often continue to sin. When we confess, we find forgiveness. Again—it's all about God and His grace.

The following thoughts were recorded after a young woman fought with her mother.

Fighting with My Mom

Tonight I hurt my mother. It's a terrible thing when you realize you've hurt someone you love. Your heart breaks with the knowledge that you have confronted love with the ugliness of hatred. In that situation, you see yourself as you are; you are ashamed.

How many times since that first fall from grace have we, like Adam and Eve, hid from the light of God's love? Why? Why do we turn from unconditional love? Because we see how unlovely we are, and cannot fathom that God loves us in the midst of our state. When pierced with the light we have two choices: to turn toward it, or away. If trapped in a cave, we saw a ray of light, we could move toward the light and thus find freedom, or remain in darkness.

I don't want to hide from my Father anymore. I can't comprehend His love for me, but I do comprehend that the times I fall and allow Him to graciously pick me up—I find myself standing on the truth that I need Him . . . always and forever.

My mother has already forgiven me, and so has my heavenly Father; unfortunately I will hurt them both again, but as I turn to them and not away, I can only hope that love is teaching me, and through it all an intimacy is formed.

—Age 25

A Blood Transfusion

In a desperate search for significance, validation, and fulfillment, we attach ourselves to money, relationships, power, and prestige . . . until one day we awake and realize we have connected ourselves to leeches. In darkness, we have reached for the closest tangible thing; however, rather than comfort and healing we find ourselves united with something that is sucking out our life. When the light is turned on, we see ourselves, empty, lifeless, deflated, and covered in leeches. The truth emerges—we are in desperate need of redemption . . .

we must receive a blood transfusion or death is our fate. Blood that is pure, without blemish or defect, is the only thing to save us from our current state of emptiness. As the eyes of our weary heart open, before us we see a Lamb; a gentle creature, who has willingly sacrificed Himself. With a last gasp of breath He whispers, Drink of this all of you. After the last drop of blood makes its way down—covering us completely—the Lamb comes to life again, but now He lives inside of us.

"For you know that it was not with perishable things such as silver or gold that you were redeemed from the empty way of life...but with the precious blood of Christ, a lamb without blemish or defect" (1 Peter 1:18).

—Age 25

Real World Is Freedom

What do I wish someone from the "real world" had told me while I was in college? Where do I begin? There is so much that I wish someone had told me. But even if they had, would I have listened? Let me just tell you straight up . . . real world life is nothing like college and the real working world is nothing like what you learned in college. It barely prepares you! Don't get me wrong, all that you learned in college and all that work you did was not in vain. It definitely gives you an edge, but the sense of security and belonging is not there when you step off the college campus. Don't get down, though. There's a new and different feeling that you can have if you open up to it . . . a sense of freedom like you've never known! You can be and do whatever you want! Literally! There are no teachers or parents or guidance counselors or RA's giving you advice on what to do. You have total freedom to make your own decisions . . . and mistakes. And believe me, there will be mistakes. But that's okay, really it is. Everyone makes them, although it may feel like you're the only bumbling idiot who just can't seem to get things done right. Mistakes are inevitable. You must learn to laugh them off but still learn from them (and the sooner you do this the better). Even if it looks like your friends have it all together and seem to having no problems jumping right into the "real world," I'd be willing to bet they're thinking the same thing about you. We all have expectations put on us by others—and ourselves—and we are so afraid of letting anyone down. Listen, you are making all of those people proud and should be making yourself proud by not letting any mistakes, insecurities, or imperfections keep you down. You will make wrong decisions. You will mess up. And you will become a smarter and more experienced person because of it. So enjoy the college life while you can . . . but get ready for the real world and all the freedom that comes with it. Enjoy the ride!

—Age 26

And though there are trials, problems, and pain, God does have a wonderful plan for each twentysomething, and He wants you to know it!

eleven

Seeking God's Plan for Your Life

God desires for all Christians to seek His will for their lives. Throughout school years, so much is predetermined. High school students deal with the decision of which college to attend. After college there are many paths that can be chosen—graduate school, work, ministry, and the choice of cities or even countries in which to live. Most twentysomethings would love to have a road map before them—a trip ticket that carefully marks each mile, tells the best, quickest, and safest route to the final chosen destination. However, there are no easy formulas for knowing the exact will of God in our lives in every single situation. God has a general plan that is discovered in the commands and principles of the Bible. This is our guide and it's filled with guidelines for showing us how to please God and get to know Him better. Knowing God's will for your life begins right now—not later on in life. If the desire to know is there, you're on the right road for knowing what it is for your life.

"I will instruct you and teach you in the way you should go; I will counsel you and watch over you" (Psalm 32:8).

God has a general plan that applies to all of us, but He also has a specific plan—a plan that includes the circumstances He permits and the individual guidance He provides. God formed each individual with unique potential to make a contribution to life. Following His total plan, general and specific, assures our maximum well-being and the greatest fulfillment of our potential not only for the present but also for all of eternity.

The first step in knowing God's will for our lives begins with knowing God, and that happens at the moment we ask Christ to come in and take control. The Holy Spirit then acts as our guide and the Bible comes alive. There is absolutely no way that a person can know God or what He desires for their lives until this step is taken.

God is primarily known through His Word. "Your word is a lamp to my feet and a light for my path" (Psalm 119:105). It stands to reason that God's Word cannot be known unless it is read. Just a thought—how much time do you spend seeking God's will through His Word?

As you spend time in the Word, you know God more intimately and build trust in Him. It is highly important not to have false pictures of what God is like. He is not a stern father who doesn't understand us or a permissive, jolly Santa Claus. God does not cater to all our whims, nor is it His desire to remove the joy of life from those who yield to Him. No one knows better than God what is best for us. Our definition of "good" is getting what we think we want, when we want it. Our desires include comfort, immediate relief, pleasure, or a sense of achievement. God does not always meet our needs and desires, but wants us to learn that true joy can be found no matter what the circumstances. And so often, as is found throughout all the stages of life, God's will may be very different from our own, but consistently and always best.

God Provides a City

My first choice of a place to live was Chicago. It is a great city for interior design and I loved the beautiful skyscrapers and the bustling people. I focused my search on this lovely city, but sent resumes to other places. I was patient, and the Lord provided me with a great job in Washington D.C. What a blessing it has been living in this city as I am surrounded by encouraging godly women, whose life and walk with the Lord mirror mine. This is such a tough, yet exciting time in life and He has given me these women to help me, encourage me, and mutually teach me, directing me back to Him when I stumble. The Lord closed the door to the city of my dreams, but opened an even greater door. He has a plan. We must be patient and trusting. He will provide.

—Age 24

Living at Home

After college, I ended up subbing at different schools and then finally got a job as a teacher's aide. I was happy about having a more permanent job but knew this was not the job I wanted, as I still didn't make enough money to live on my own—I was living with my parents. All my friends had moved away or were starting their new jobs. I felt very alone and became depressed.

I resigned as a teacher's aide and was called that very day by the principle of another school, with the offer of the teaching position I had wanted from the beginning of my search. Words cannot express my excitement! I thanked God for leading me to this job and helping me figure out what I really did want. It's amazing to see how God's plan takes us for such an emotional ride. What I understand now is that God doesn't answer all of our prayers for a reason. We have to be patient and trust Him. He will never let us down.

After obtaining my new job I was able to move into an apartment with one of my friends. Everything started falling into place for me. And guess what? In retrospect, I do appreciate my time living at home. It gave me a chance to reflect on my life and see what I really wanted. My parents were very supportive, helping as much as they could while I gained tremendous independence and knew that I was now responsible for my own happiness and success in my career. No matter how difficult life feels after the excitement of graduation wears off, know that God's plan is in action and the results will leave you so happy.

—Age 25

"Wait for the LORD; be strong and take heart and wait for the LORD" (Psalm 27:14). God always answers our prayers in one of three ways: "yes," "no," or "wait"! Waiting is often the hardest to accept and yet this is the time when patience is built most deeply. When God asks us to surrender our personal plans or preferences, He always has something better. Surrender to Him never makes us less than we want to be, but so much more than we are able to envision for ourselves.

"In his heart a man plans his course, but the LORD determines his steps" (Proverbs 16:9). Am I willing to accept God's will for my life if it is not what I had in mind? Am I willing to accept His will for my life even if I don't know what it is? Until I am willing to accept and obey—God will not show me His will.

Trust God to make His will known or bring us into His will. God does not want us to worry but to trust Him to bring us to where He wants us to be. And in knowing God's will, know that His will isn't a one-time situation. He cares as much about the process of our life as He does the final production.

Longing for Home

In your careers—be patient. It may take a couple of jobs to figure our what you want to do. This is normal—do not get frustrated. Some jobs may require you to move to another city, and that can be fun too. Just look at it as an adventure. I must tell you, after I moved away for a year, I found myself longing to be back home. I was a little embarrassed to tell my friends because I thought they would think that I was a homebody. However, I moved home and have never regretted it.

Don't ever be embarrassed about wanting to return home where your family is. The older I've gotten, the more I've learned that when you have nothing else or no one else, you have your family. I see my grandparents getting older, and my parents, and there's just something to be said about spending time with them. One day we'll look back and wish we could have had just a little more time with them (for those living away, holidays are a great time to be with family). You know, a lifetime is a long time, but it is short at the same time.

—Age 26

If we are resisting God's plan, any happiness we are able to squeeze from life by going our own way will be marred by inner conflict. On the other hand, God's plan for our life, which is always good, includes ever-increasing deliverance from emotions that rob us of our joy—the distress of feeling we never quite measure up, the fears of what people think of us as well as the inability to accept ourselves.

Finding God's will means taking the steps that you can. Ask God to block a decision if it is not His will. "Whoever watches the wind will not plant; whoever looks at the clouds will not reap"

(Ecclesiastes 11:4). And in the "real world," perfect conditions are a rarity, as explained by this young woman.

Big-City Life

In college your days are filled with people—people you know or at least recognize their faces. In the "real world" that isn't necessarily so—especially if you choose your new hometown to be New York City. Going to a new place can really be a challenge. For instance, you have to make the effort to even see someone you know. After working hard all day, sometimes it would be so nice just to come home to familiar friends living in the same neighborhood or the same building. Although the big-city experience sounds glamorous and exciting—it is something that takes hard work and time. If this is your dream—go for it! At first I was overwhelmed but after a few months I can say that this experience has greatly enriched my life. I'm so glad I did it. I'm so much stronger.

—Age 23

Pray for specific direction, as prayer is the key to knowing God's will. God gains access to our thoughts when we pray. How much time do you spend in prayer to God? How much do you desire to know His will? And timing is a big part of God's plan.

Step Out in Faith

When I moved to DC I didn't have a job. I was so worried about living there and paying rent with no income. But I just knew I was supposed to go. The day I moved in I got a call from home that my best friend's father had died from a sudden heart attack. I immediately went back home the next day. Because I had no obligations in DC yet (job) I was able to spend the entire week with my friend. It was a tremendous blessing. The day I arrived back in DC I had an e-mail from one of my prospective job contacts—they had an opening. I interviewed the next day and started work a week later. The timing was perfect. Had I gotten the job any earlier I wouldn't have been able to spend such a long time at home. God saw the whole picture, knew every detail, and provided for me according to His impeccable plan, not to my anxiety-ridden hopes and timing. Rest in His promises and trust in His love. He sees the big picture and knows better than we do. Step out in faith and rest in the knowledge that He is in control.

—Age 24

There will be times when we honestly just don't know what to do. This is the time to seek wise counsel from those who love you and are actively seeking God's will for their own lives. "For lack of guidance a nation falls, but many advisers make victory sure" (Proverbs 11:14).

In Between Jobs

Several months went by and I hit a wall. I had recently lost my father, I did not have a job, finances were beginning to run low, friends were getting married or moving to more exciting places, and all of those doors that I once thought were so open seemed to be slamming shut. In desperation I called my pastor and told him my state. His response: "Read your Bible, pray, exercise." Things I knew to do, simple things, yet words I needed to be reminded of.

It has been six months since I finished my college career and entered into the "real world." I start my first job in six days. I feel relief to have a job, which brings security and independence. However, my security is really stemming from taking my pastor's advice. So what have I learned from these six months? A relationship with Christ, and all that comes with that, including Bible reading, prayer, church, and fellow-ship, must be the first step before the next step is a good step. Because, truthfully, not much has changed—I still am left without a father, my friends are still getting married and moving to more exciting places, and a lot of doors are contin-uing to remain closed—yet I am allowing God to be the guide now.

—Age 24

Avoid premature conclusions. At times God uses circumstances to point us in the right direction, but that is not always the case. A rule of thumb is to make certain that everything squares up with God's Word. God's will never includes anything that goes against His Word.

And God's will for our lives does include heartache and prob-lems. Trials are sent to test us—to make us stronger. And when hard times come our way, it is reassuring to know that God's hand is still upon us. Nothing comes into our lives without the express permission of God. "And we know that in all things God works for the good of those who love him, who have been called according to his purpose" (Romans 8:28). To know God's will and do it is the key to a happy, successful life as Jesus exemplified by His own life.

God wants us to know His will! We do not have to play hide and seek. As we yield to God's plan for our lives, and let Him work within us, the uniqueness of our lives will unfold and our very being will be a significant contribution of fulfillment, which brings great glory and pleasure to God. This gives true meaning and success to all that we are and all that we do.

G *twelve*

Getting Involved

"*Y*ou are the salt of the earth. But if the salt loses its saltiness, how can it be made salty again? It is no longer good for anything, except to be thrown out and trampled by men. You are the light of the world. A city on a hill cannot be hidden. Neither do people light a lamp and put it under a bowl. Instead they put it on its stand, and it gives light to everyone in the house. In the same way, let your light shine before men, that they may see your good deeds and praise your Father in heaven."

—Matthew 5:13-16

These verses not only describe the character of a Christian but also show how to apply this description. Christians are called to be in the world but not of the world—to be examples to those who do not believe, and to make a difference in all situations.

We live in a fallen world—filled with sorrow, sickness, and sin. The world needs help and Christians are called to be salt and light—to help bring healing, wholeness, and wholesomeness. Just as meat tends to spoil without salt, so the "real world" becomes spoiled apart from the gospel and God's grace. Salt goes a long way. It makes a difference with only a little bit being used. Salt purifies and provides flavor. Twentysomethings can make a tremendous difference in their relationships and circumstances. And this becomes a reality through involvement—through reaching out, encouraging others and in the same way being encouraged also.

Get Involved

I think it is important to get involved. Whatever city you end up in—whether it is your hometown or a new city—meet people. Get out and find a group to go to church, join a church, join a civic organization, get out and meet people. This is more difficult now because there are not dorms, sororities, etc., but it is so important. The world can be a lonely place if you don't surround yourself with friends and most importantly Christian friends. It is important to meet friends that like you for who you are, what you believe, and the fact that you stick to it.

—Age 27

Build Relationships

Get connected and build relationships. Make this a priority in prayer and seek out friendships that will be an encouragement to you. I made the mistake of not making this a priority and instead focused constantly on my job. I went through tough adjustments in my life after college. However, if I had made it a priority to build relationships, I believe the transition would have been easier for me! And most important is my personal relationship with Jesus Christ—it's not the act of going to church or doing things for Him daily, but it is my time alone with Him and building of my relationship with Him that has been my constant strength and anchor to keep me on the straight path of His plan for my life.

—Age 25

Without Christ, the world would be in a state of darkness. Life only makes sense when it is lived for God. The Westminster Shorter Catechism states—"The chief end of man is to glorify God and enjoy Him forever." How do we glorify God? Our lives should always be the first thing to speak. If our lips speak more than our lives, it will mean very little! Jesus is the light of the world. "When Jesus spoke again to the people, he said, 'I am the light of the world. Whoever follows me will never walk in darkness, but will have the light of life'" (John 8:12).

But He also says "you are the light of the world" (vs. 14). We are ambassadors for Christ. And what does light do? It exposes darkness. If I am living my life as Jesus wants me to, I will show others who do not believe that there is something missing in their own life.

A Blessing to Coworkers

Know what you believe in and stand up for it. Right out of college I took a job as a flight attendant and was based out of Oakland, California. I was thrown into a very secular environment—only about 10% of the population in the San Francisco Bay area goes to church. So I would be safe to say, nine times out of ten, I was working three- and four-day trips with girls and guys who were not Christians. This was a great opportunity to minister into the lives of these coworkers who need the Lord. If I had been willing to party and sleep around, I could have done it with someone different every night of the week. Thank the Lord, He had shown me what to do and what not to do by this point in my life.

—Age 26

Lamps are not meant to be hidden. Jesus is the lampstand. But Christians glorify God as they are willing to let their lives shine before men. All good is meant for God's glory—not our own accolades.

What does it mean to glorify God? "If anyone speaks, he should do it as one speaking the very words of God. If anyone serves, he should do it with the strength God provides, so that in all things God may be praised through Jesus Christ. To him be the glory and the power for ever and ever. Amen" (1 Peter 4:11). In order to stand strong in the "real world," it is important to stay filled with the power of the Holy Spirit. A support group of like-minded people is an asset, and getting involved with a local church is of such importance.

Find a Church

If you relocate to a new place, be sure and make it a top priority to find a home church as soon as possible. This will make you feel like you have a family away from home. This way you can surround yourself with believers at some point each week through Sunday worship and through a small group Bible study.

—Age 26

Christian Support

My advice for the young woman entering the real world would be to get involved with a church family. Surround yourself with a Christian support group and draw closer to

God. That will help you face all of the secular lifestyles that a work environment will introduce to you. It will also help you find God's will for your life, which is the perfect plan.

—Age 23

Take the Initiative

I personally benefited from a solid Bible teaching church but I couldn't get plugged into a singles group. Somehow, bowling and ice cream socials weren't meeting my needs. You will have to take the initiative to find your place, and don't wait for someone to come find you.

—Age 28

Volunteer

When moving to a new city and starting life in the real world, finding a not-for-profit that is a good fit for you is one of the best ways to make a difference and meet people. When I moved to New York City the first thing I did was research the not-for-profits in the area—there are about a million different causes. I found one that really interested me and a cause that I was passionate about and volunteered. It wasn't a lot of time, but it feels good to give back. This year I have added another charity to my roster. I have met some of the coolest people and made good business connections as well.

—Age 24

Don't Be Overinvolved

It is so hard to find time to be alone. Work occupies all of my day, as well as many nights and weekends. When I am not working, I am out with friends, or too tired to think, and I sit in front of the TV for some downtime before bed. My health has suffered from my lack of sleep and busy schedule, and so has my relationship with the Lord. My day is in balance when I take time in the morning to "be still" and listen. It is important to say no sometimes, and make sure to make it a priority to refresh your mind and renew your spirit through daily study and prayer. The difference is so amazing, yet I often rush from place to place, become frazzled, and forget how much more full and peaceful my life is when I am in tune with God.

—Age 24

thirteen

The Ins and Outs of Jobs

Recently I was leading a retreat for senior girls at Washington and Lee University in Lexington, Virginia. One of the young women handed me a copy of the May 7, 2003, issue of their school newspaper, *The Trident.* The headline read: "W&L seniors are struggling to find employment." Many students, after four years of hard work, several summer internships, and many interviews were still searching for a job. The article continued:

"Indeed, data show that graduating students do not have as many options. According to an annual survey conducted by Dr. Phil Gardner, director of the Collegiate Employment Research Institute and associate director of career services at Michigan State University, companies are not planning to hire as many new graduates compared to previous years. Companies expressed decreased optimism in the confidence of the college labor market compared to last year. In fact, fewer than 30 percent of respondents plan to hire new graduates this year compared to about 35 percent of firms hiring last year. According to the National Association of Colleges and Employers, an organization that keeps statistics on the job market, 'employers blame the shrinking number of job opportunities for members of the class of 2003 on diminishing needs, on their organizations having fewer clients requiring services, budgetary cutbacks, hiring freezes, low attrition, and layoffs.'

Many students who have recently graduated from college and have been thrown into the "real world" are not handling it well. Many are angry and depressed, wanting only to go back to college. One graduate says, 'It was programmed in my head that I deserved the job I wanted. When I finally got a job working five days a week, I was like, 'That is it, this is what I'm going to do for the rest of my life?' Um, yeah. Welcome, again, to the real world" (quoted in *Denver Post*, January. 6, 2003).

When gathering data for this book, I realized that the response on this subject was overwhelming. Finding a job, finding a job you like, keeping a job, balancing a job with life, coping with a job—these were just a few of the new dynamics in the "real world."

Not So Great

I wish someone had told me that my first job was not necessarily going to be great! After all that work in graduate school, I had hoped to be able to go to work and let those idealistic and change-the-world notions flourish. However, I found my first job to be discouraging and filled with a staff of people who were burned out. But I always thought you were supposed to stay at a job for at least a year, so I stuck it out.

—Age 27

First Job Not Forever

Once you have accepted a job, just remember that it is your FIRST job. It does not have to be forever. It is okay to not like it! In fact, you probably won't! Do not be afraid to find something else. If you really know what you want to do, call anyone and everyone who could help you make it happen. Use any contacts or leads to get the job you want. Do not be afraid to ask people for help. They were once looking for a job too. In the end, you just have to trust that God has a plan for us and He will always take care of you.

—Age 28

Try It Out

Try spending the summers traveling or doing internships in different cities or countries.

There are so many careers that you would never even think possible until you get out and see the marketplace. Internships are a great way to try out different careers before you actually commit to one, as well as a great way to network.

—Age 28

Regrets of a Gofer

I wanted to be a mom since I can remember. When friends talked of dreams of law and medicine, banking, etc., I could not relate but would always throw out some bogus career just to go along. So declaring a major second year of college proved quite difficult. A child development-type degree was all that sparked my interest. Nevertheless, finding a job to financially support me was a struggle. My boyfriend and I were in love but in no hurry to marry, and I was determined to have a couple of years of independence before sharing a checking account. So my career as mom was years away.

For my first job out of college, I was hired as the office assistant for a company not related to my major, but with exciting opportunities. My duties were filling in for the receptionist, mail, maintaining supplies, and several other chores that seemed so menial. I quit three months later. I wish someone had reminded me that everyone has to start at the bottom, even with a college degree. Had I kept a good attitude and stuck with that position for just a little while longer, my hard work would have paid off as I moved up the corporate ladder. Instead I went through 5 jobs in 4 years before landing the job of my dreams. The two lessons I learned from that experience are that you are not required to know what you want to do for the rest of your life when you declare a major and that everyone starts out as a gofer—stay with it and your hard work will pay off.

—Age 28

Respect for Your Employer

I'm still undecided if there is such a thing as a perfect job. I do believe that if you do not respect the person and the company that you work for then you're in store for a lot of trouble. If you can't talk about your job or the company you work for with pride (even if you're an assistant to an assistant), then you need to reevaluate why it is that you're at that company.

—Age 24

Never Lie in Business

Never lie in business. You'll see people who do it all the time and get away with it and make a lot more money than those who tell the truth. Don't even think about compromising any

personal standards to "get ahead" in the working world. It's
not worth it and people who get by doing that only get so far.
—Age 24

So maybe there is no "perfect" job, but it is probable that a job which
demands that you compromise your beliefs is not the place to be.
The headlines of today prove that fact to be true as more and more
large corporations are collapsing due to greed, fraud, and deceit.
You never have to do anything illegal or unethical. Respect is hard
to come by and easily lost. When starting a new job, you must prove
yourself. Don't lose that good reputation.

It's also important to be careful concerning relationships and
friendships with coworkers. Always be polite and respectful—cau-
tious about what you say and how you act, especially toward the
opposite sex.

Dating at Work

If you like your job and do not want to leave, never date
someone from work. This rarely ends well and can be very
awkward. Jealousy is an ugly thing.

—Age 23

Married Men

I never thought I would be faced with a situation where I
would potentially cause a married man to stumble. We are
surrounded by people of different ages, and often work
closely with them. I have always been naïve when it comes to
thinking that a married man would ever come on to me, but
it has happened too many times, to me and my friends. We
must be aware that we are at the prime of our lives. It is dangerous to be alone with a married man, even if you think
nothing of it. Chances are, many times the man is hoping

something might happen. Be aware when you are alone with a man, and evaluate why you are there and what good could come out of it.

Be Different

Though many people might not agree with your faith, I've learned that they accept it, but more importantly, those who are scared to talk about their faith feel more comfortable sharing if you open up first. The way we live either underlines or crosses out all that we say.

—Age 24

Kindness

I started my job search by applying for internships but much to my dismay received a position that was my last choice. Several people had warned me not to pursue this program at all. After just a few short hours of my first day, I understood why every intern before me had complained, left, or cried. My boss was completely unethical, and extremely picky. Nothing was ever perfect, and everything had to be completed very quickly. However, for some reason or another, I welcomed the lack of compassion, and greeted it with open arms—something this person had never experienced or knew how to handle. Several times I was asked questions by Human Resources, as to how my internship was going, and every time I fought back the urge to say what I really thought, and instead said "just fine." It wasn't that I didn't want to stand up for myself, it was just the simple fact that if I expressed my true thoughts, just as everyone before me had so willingly done, nothing would have changed. Every person before me complained, and it didn't help them, so why was I going to allow myself to do the same, setting myself up for the disappointment of

being reprimanded by my boss once they heard what was said? After all, what made my arguments any different? So I decided to take a different angle, and boy did it work!
—Age 24

This young woman made the decision to treat others as better than herself. She figured that God knew what she was going through and she chose to be thankful for what she had rather than complain about what she did not have. After all, it is so much easier for someone to have a great attitude when things are going well for them. She continued, "I felt like everyone around me was just waiting for me to explode out of complete frustration. For that very reason I made it my mission to have an enthusiastic approach."

What happened? At the end of her internship her boss said she was the best intern they had had in over 15 years. She was hired on the spot and received the highest starting salary allowed, along with several large responsibilities. Everything she had worked so hard to achieve fell into place, and of course, everyone in the office was stunned and amazed at what had been accomplished. "No matter how people above me may appear unappreciative of my efforts, I push forward and constantly remind myself that my purpose is not to please others but to please God. I try to focus on the eternal perspective instead of a worldly one—knowing that the office world is also a place to please God. Thus, the bar is raised, and my work is better when He is in control of my projects, attitude and life." This young woman stayed in an unpleasant job, became a witness for her faith, and in the end was rewarded by her company.

Miserable Job

I decided to leave the job that made me miserable. I do not think God wants us to be miserable! Each day on earth is for us to love God and love others. I was not doing that. I wanted to find something where I felt God's peace. I wanted to follow my heart and God's direction for my life, not worrying about the opinions of others.

—Age 27

The Dreaded Job Search

When I got home from East Asia, I was where most people are when they graduate from college....I began the dreaded job search! No one told me how emotional and draining that process can be. I prayed and prayed that God would open a door for me somewhere. A mistake I almost made was accepting the first job I was offered. I was so tired of looking that I just wanted the search to be over. I guess I lost sight of the fact that God had a job prepared for me and I didn't need to quit until I knew I had found it. Thankfully, I had supportive parents to help me out financially as I interviewed, waited, and prayed. God ended up opening up a position at a Children's Hospital and I could not have asked for a better fit for me. I definitely learned something about patience and perseverance during that time.

—Age 26

Take a Break

Not realizing I could negotiate a "start date," I offered my availability for the first day after I completed graduate school. I suppose I thought that I would never find another job, or that somehow they would hire someone else, because I couldn't start that very week. Both of those thoughts were not true, and as time went on, I realized that it was not as urgent as it seemed. If they really want and need you for the position, one more week (or perhaps more) is not unreasonable. If only I had known. I did learn my lesson, however, and a few years later when I changed jobs, I allowed for a full week to travel, relax, and just enjoy the break!

—Age 29

Find a Mentor

Find a mentor—someone you can respect who is on a similar career path. This person should be older enough than you are to have had more working and life experiences. When I moved to New York, one of the senior women in the company took me under her wing. Her career is star-studded and she is someone that I admire personally and professionally. I felt comfortable asking her questions at work and she gave me advice on how to reach my career goals.

—Age 24

In today's economy, you must set yourself apart from your competition. Find creative ways to get the attention of employers. "Graduating with accolades is great, but simply won't cut it today," a 25-year-old emphasizes. "Determination and persistence will eventually pay off. Keep an optimistic and upbeat attitude."

At the same time, it is wise not to get so caught up in the rat race of success that your job causes you to miss out on all the other things that life has to offer.

Racing with Rats

I am a competitive person, so it was easy to get caught up in succeeding in my job. You have to be conscious that your success is not measured by a paycheck or a bonus. It is more important to like what you are doing and have fun doing it. I think guys can fall into the rat race trap more easily than girls, but the temptation is still there.

—Age 25

Give Yourself Time

When I started my job I was full of energy, ready to work, happy to stay late, and wanting to learn as much as I could, but I felt so ignorant for the first three months and started doubting my abilities. After talking to some friends, I realized that those feelings were completely natural. No one is expected to know everything about their job at the beginning.

—Age 25

And you'll never know what you can do unless you try. When looking for a job, don't think you have to have the right major for a particular job or field. A 24-year-old New Yorker explains, "I was an English and French major and yet I got a job in PR and event planning. There were no French clients and not much writing was involved. I ended up doing parties for the Golden Globes, Emmys, and Oscars. Now I work for a major magazine, never having had one journalism class." She goes on to explain that many people told her she would never get a job in the media as it is too competitive—not to mention the fact that she had no experience or proper college majors. "I'm glad I didn't limit myself by listening to the advice of others!"

Another 24-year-old was working at a restaurant where she had been employed during summers and holiday breaks from school. She enjoyed her job and the friends she had there but felt that she was not being used to her fullest potential. "I remember that day perfectly. I stood quietly at the hostess stand and decided to pray. I asked God to open a door for me so I might feel I was doing something worthwhile. I had no idea that thirty minutes later the man who walked into the restaurant would be my future boss." Through small talk, the man told her about his new restaurant that had just opened and indicated that he was looking for a new manager. That was her degree! "Everything he mentioned was what I was looking for. I went home that night ecstatic! How faithful is our Lord?"

At times God uses past experiences to direct us to a job for which we have great passion. After six months of interviewing with no success, the self-esteem of a 24-year-old took a nosedive. Great grades and compliments from teachers were replaced by rejection letters and dead-end streets. Then she heard about a job opening with the American Cancer Society and it changed everything. Several years before, one of her good friends with whom she had spend thirteen years of school was diagnosed with acute myelogenous leukemia. For ten months the battle was waged but after a short-lived remission, she and her family were forced to make a decision between going through chemotherapy again, which had been so hard on her body, or letting the cancer take its course. The battle was lost to cancer. "A job fighting cancer deeply appealed to me. I had gotten a taste of what it felt like to help get rid of something that killed people so senselessly by being a part of the Leukemia Society's Team In Training Program." In her interview she told the regional vice president, "I know what people who are dying with cancer look like, what they go through, and I am willing to do whatever it takes to get rid of this evil disease."

There is something that you are supposed to do in this life. There is a purpose you are here to fulfill and you may have absolutely no idea what it is. But always trust God that it is there. Interviewers may say "no" but there will be that right door. And when you walk through it, you will find a place where you are needed—the unique you. It may surprise you to see where you end up! But you will be able to make your mark and have a great impact on the lives of others and bring glory to God as well.

fourteen

Finances

"The youth of our generation have basically been spoiled and they don't feel comfortable dealing with adversity because they were raised with a cornucopia of material resources and expect it to continue....When they do face adversity they have difficulty responding. The baby boomers have had a successful economic run and have not taught their children to go without or to struggle."

—*Denver Post,* January 6, 2003

Money makes the world go around. So often I have heard the quote—"a woman can never be too rich or too thin." Ours is a very materialistic society. Many college students have never had to support themselves financially and know very little about money until they hit the "real world." Learning to budget and manage your own money can be very challenging. And even more challenging can be the fact that many women choose to move to a city where the cost of living is extraordinary. How important to remember to live within your means! That means to spend only the amount that you make each month—and no more.

Pay No Interest

Do not get credit cards if you have a tendency to run up the bill and not be able to pay them off at the end of every single month. Let it be your goal to not let a single credit card company get one dime from you in interest!

—Age 26

The Drag of Debt

I have more friends who brought $20,000 worth of credit card debt into their new marriages after being out of college for several years. Now, many years later, they are still trying to get rid of debt and find it impossible to save enough for a down payment on a house or condominium.

—Age 26

So what happens when you try to live within your means and see some of your friends buying houses, shopping at nice stores, driving nice cars, etc.? This may cause a huge struggle within or without, especially if you are married.

Start Saving Money

Start saving money in college. I wish someone had told me to put $20 away a week or even $50 a month. If I had put a mere $50 a month away for the 4 years of college, I would have had $2500 to start out in the "real world." It's not enough to buy a house but almost enough for a deposit and

first month's rent in New York City. I encourage you to keep a
budget, and write down everything you spend.

—Age 24

There are many individuals who have lived in the real world for a long time and understand the ins and outs of finances. Don't be afraid to seek out their wisdom in the areas of finance and investments.

I believe that gathering information from many people
gave me a lot of great information and helped me make
smart decisions in a timely manner regarding my finances,
retirement plan, savings, and housing.

—Age 25

What about transportation? If you live in a big city, may not have to worry about this, as public transit systems may work so well. Many young people receive cars as graduation gifts after finishing college. Others may already have a car. The choice is totally individual and dictated by circumstances, living situation, and finances. Whatever you decide, think it through as this 23-year-old has done in a most excellent fashion.

Buying a Car

Okay, buying a car. That is what most people want to do
after college. DO NOT. Decide how much you want to
spend on a car. Make the payments to yourself. When you
have the money saved, you can either use the money you
would have spent on interest by upgrading your car or
using the money on a vacation. Just drive your car until it
dies. My car is 10 years old, still running. You have the rest
of your life to drive a nice car. You don't need one now.

I also do not suggest leasing a car. What do you have at the end of the lease? Nothing, no car. You have no collateral, no equity. I know leases usually require less of a down payment and less payment, but it is not an investment. Buying a two- or three-year-old car is better, but not in every case. Some cars hold their value. The day you drive a car off the lot, it depreciates. Just do your research. Other money advice is: if you save from age 25–35 $400 a month and let it sit in an account until you retire at age 55, you will have more money than if you saved from age 35–55 $400 a month. Ten years or 20 years. Interest pays.

—Age 23

Almost everyone feels that they aren't making enough money to live on as they first enter the real world. Everything has a price and added together those things can seem like a fortune. Entry-level positions can be tough.

So how do I fit God into this equation? Jesus had a lot to say about the subject of money. In fact He spoke about it more than any other subject. Along with speaking about money, many warnings were given. That is only logical as throughout the centuries people have killed for it, died for it, and lusted for it. Money has caused much heartache, torn millions of marriages apart, separated the best of friends, and caused the demise of many who were proud and mighty.

"For where your treasure is, there your heart will be also" (Matthew 6:21). God has riches available for all His children. All that we have is from God and we can show that we love God by giving of ourselves, our time, our possessions, our talents, and our money as well. Giving is sharing what God has given to us. We can never out-give God for as we give, He will continue to give back to us. God promises that if we sow bountifully, we will reap abundantly! Even extravagant giving is honored by God. He honors His promise concerning generosity. "Whoever sows sparingly will also reap sparingly, and whoever sows generously will also reap generously" (2 Corinthians 9:6).

Giving to God

I have learned the hard way at times that it pays to give your first 10% to the Lord. Everything belongs to Him anyway! But it amazes me that as I faithfully give to Him first, He always meets my needs above and beyond what I could fathom. Oftentimes, I have balanced my checkbook and realized that there is no way that God could financially tide me over until the next paycheck because on paper it doesn't work out. However, God always blesses me and I have never ever run out of money, putting God first. He is the ultimate balance of checkbooks. I am not saying that I have had lots of money lying around; often God makes it a close call, but He always comes through. The key is understanding the principal that when you don't share in giving back to the Lord's work, you have a hold on your money and your possessions. When you give God your very first 10%, you are acknowledging His power and control in your life over everything that you have. That way you are acknowledging Him as being in control of all of your possessions, and you are outwardly saying, "Lord, I trust You with my life and money and all of my stuff!" That is huge and pleases God's heart greatly.

—Age 24

God wants us to give cheerfully—not because we have to. "'Do not store up for yourselves treasures on earth, where moth and rust destroy, and where thieves break in and steal. But store up for yourselves treasures in heaven, where moth and rust do not destroy,

and where thieves do not break in and steal. For where your treasure is, there your heart will be also" (Matthew 6:19–21). Material
wealth will be destroyed where spiritual wealth will last forever.
Where is my heart? What do I place the most emphasis on? What is
my treasure?

My Own Money

When I started my job, it was the first time in life that I had
my own money coming in on a consistent basis. I grew up
watching my parents tithe and did so myself on occasion
when I had money. However, I didn't realize the importance
of it until I started working. Most jobs right out of college are
not the highest paying jobs, so it was tempting to pay all of
my bills and then give my tithe at the end of the month. Over
time, God taught me that this was His money that He had
entrusted to me and that I needed to take that 10% out of
my paycheck as soon as I got it. I needed to trust that God
would provide for me each month, rather than holding onto
my money as a security blanket. (It's funny—looking back
now, I realize that as I changed my habits, over the next year
and a half, I got 4 raises! Not that He will give us a raise every
time we are obedient, but I just thought it was cool.) It really
has been amazing to learn that God longs to bless us. And as
we are obedient, and give back to Him, He blesses us even
more. It really is freeing and will revolutionize your life and
your take on finances as you begin to give. I have learned that
anytime I feel a notion that I should give money to a charity,
a ministry, or even to a person on the street, to not think
twice. I guess this is all a part of a process of learning to hold
on loosely to the things of the world and truly realize God is
the provider and that He longs to bless us!

—Age 26

Jesus warns us not to be greedy. Possessions do not last forever and do not constitute a man's worth. "Then he said to them, 'Watch out! Be on your guard against all kinds of greed; a man's life does not consist in the abundance of his possessions'" (Luke 12:15).

"In everything I did, I showed you that by this kind of hard work we must help the weak, remembering the words the Lord Jesus himself said: 'It is more blessed to give than to receive'" (Acts 20:35). Do I feel that way? Do I give because I have to or because I want to? Do I give just to get? If that is the case, you'll always lose. God delights in generous givers and He will personally give them everything they need.

> "*But* seek first his kingdom and his righteousness, and all these things will be given to you as well."
>
> —Matthew 6:33

Jesus wants not only our money but our time, possessions, talents. He wants it all.

fifteen

Careers and Ministry

The world tells us that if we want to lead, be successful, have prestige, and be happy, we must look out for number one! However,
Jesus tells us just the opposite. He teaches that to lead is to serve,
and this service is to the glory of God. "Do nothing out of selfish
ambition or vain conceit, but in humility consider others better
than yourselves. 4Each of you should look not only to your own
interests, but also to the interests of others" (Philippians 2:3–4).

Jesus came to serve without giving up His leadership. He is
our greatest example of a servant. He did not pretend to be a servant. He was one. Christ "made himself nothing, taking the very
nature of a servant, being made in human likeness. And being
found in appearance as a man, he humbled himself and became
obedient to death—even death on a cross!" (Philippians 2:7–8).

Thinking of others is not enough. Christians are called to
serve, and that involves sacrifice. Many people are willing to serve if

it doesn't cost them anything. What are we willing to sacrifice?

The "real world" offers real opportunities for service. Sometimes God calls people to extremely sacrificial situations. For this 26-year-old, this meant leaving the comfort of the United States and becoming a missionary to the people of East Asia.

A Missionary Year

About halfway through my senior year, I started thinking about life beyond college. The more I thought about the future, it began to excite me more and scare me less. I began to realize what a blank slate I had. I honestly think that the first year after you graduate presents such a unique opportunity. It is the only time in life that you are not tied down to anything. I didn't have a job yet, so I didn't have to worry about vacation days. I wasn't married, so I didn't have that limiting my number of choices. And all of my best friends were going to be moving to about 5 different cities in the south, so we wouldn't all be together no matter what decision I made. The more I prayed about it, I found the Lord leading me to commit to spending a year as a missionary in East Asia. It wasn't like I had this major burden on my heart for the people of East Asia, but there was a group going from my school and I thought, why not? There was nothing and no one holding me back. It was out of my comfort zone and I knew God would use it to change me as well as those around me. At first I didn't really love the people or feel a calling to share the gospel with them. It ended up being the most amazing year of my life as the Lord broke and refined me in ways I never knew I even needed. Somehow God really draws you to Himself when you take the step to get away from all that is familiar to you and He is all you have.

—Age 26

There's a paradox here. The more we give—the more God blesses. The goal of everything we do should be to glorify God. Sacrifice and service will lead to glory. "Humble yourselves, therefore, under God's mighty hand, that he may lift you up in due time" (1 Peter 5:6). The role and lifestyle of every Christian, and that includes being "twentysomething," is to serve and be others-centered. The Greek word for minister means "to serve." We can choose to be self-centered or others-centered.

I was considering taking a job as a short-term missionary inside the United States. I wanted to go where God was leading, but thought God had confused me with someone else. I prayed, "Surely, God, this is not what You want me to do. I am not cut out for working with the poor. I don't think I have the strength to stay positive while working with people living in such hopeless situations. Isn't that a recipe for unhappiness? Don't You see me in a more fun, exciting job where I have fewer elements stacked against me?"

After a lot of prayer I began to feel God urge me to let go of my fear. I went to another city to begin a two-year journey, thinking that trusting God and making the decision to accept that position would be the hardest part. That was not the case. My time as a short-term missionary was filled with sorrow, joy, frustration, love, anger, friendship, and at times, despair. It was quite a journey. It taught me countless things, among the most important being a new insight into trusting God. There were plenty of times during the two years when I would think, "God, are You sure You want me here—this is much harder than what I had in mind!" The still, reassuring voice (that I was afraid was my imagination) was on several occasions the only thing that kept me from packing up my bags and taking the first flight home.

I had to learn to trust God even through the parts that I considered terrible. I had to learn to believe that there was a greater goodness that would result from a lot of unpleasantness. And of course, in retrospect, the most important things that God showed me during those two years came from both the good times and the really hard times.

Some of the things that God shows us cannot be found in joy. And, conversely, some of the lessons cannot be found in sorrow. We must have both. That is why, ultimately, the range of emotions that are life should hold no fear for us. I believe that there is nothing that God cannot use for good, eventually—somehow. It may take months or years for that goodness to become apparent to our human eyes, but the potential is always there.

My two-year experience was not one that I would have ever picked out for myself, but I am grateful that God led me into it. It was a precious time of growth for my heart and my mind. I am thankful that it is not up to me to handpick my experiences. Without God's direction, I would surely miss out on some of the best opportunities.

There is no verse in the Bible that says that if you follow Christ, you will not have sorrow, pain, difficulty, and loss. But the really weird part, the part that does not make any sense to our brains, is that sometimes the difficult times can show you a world of good that you otherwise would not find. I am not advocating that we be gluttons for punishment—seeking out unhappiness is not my recommendation! But the simple fact is that difficult times will come. I think the trick is trusting God through those difficulties, and letting God use those difficult times to show us something greater.

—Age 27

This 27-year-old became involved with homeless women at the age of 13. She now realizes that it was God who led her there and God who keeps leading her back to this population—even on days when she gets into her car saying, "I will never work with the homeless again."

The Real World Is God's World

What the "real world" means to me is letting God have ultimate control of my life, and listening to His call. The real world is so genuine, sacred, and overpowering because it is God's world and I am so blessed to know Him and live within His kingdom. I do not believe there is a formula or specific process for living in God's real world. Many times I try to conquer the world on my own and almost immediately goof, falling flat on the ground, realizing that I am at the mercy of Jesus Christ. I realize daily that anything I try to do without Jesus Christ as my consultant, I am at an utter loss. I think about all the times I go to others for consultation, advice, and opinions, when if I spent one tenth of that time going to Jesus for guidance and counsel, I would be in a much better place!

—Age 27

The happiest and most fulfilled person you know is most likely the most caring, unselfish, serving person you know also. Serving and helping others can help you lose your own problems.

After working with the homeless for 14 years, this young woman speaks—

God's Mission

The saying "I am on a mission" is one I have tried to erase from my vocabulary because it is God's mission that I am on—not my own. He is the ultimate one and only missionary, and I am

His servant—the arms and legs that carry out His mission. I have realized that the carrying out of His mission needs to be everywhere—from the neighborhood party at the country club to unreached peoples in Nepal. Therefore, our professional lives can and must involve Christ whether we work in a suit in a high-powered corporation, or in jeans at the soup kitchen. I imagine some people think the real servants are those in the trenches of social work with God's underprivileged people, but the Good News is for all people—and praise be to God that we are all His precious children—sins and all!

—Age 24

And it is true—the country club, the workout center, the office, etc. are all mission fields. Since many people never go to church, read the Bible, or pray, the only way they may ever discover the love and forgiveness of Jesus is by seeing Him in your life. God uses people everywhere. It helps to keep this in mind no matter where you find yourself. God is using you for His glory. Ask Him to show you how He can use you—no matter how insignificant you may think it is. "If anyone would come after me, he must deny himself and take up his cross daily and follow me. For whoever wants to save his life will lose it, but whoever loses his life for me will save it" (Luke 9:23-24).

Jesus tells us that He loves us and will provide for all of our needs. Our responsibility is to turn everything over to Him to do with as He sees fit. This is not always easy, as we want to run our lives the way we see fit. Remember—obedience always leads to blessings. If we put God's interests first He promises to give us everything we need.

It's in the Journey

I had been seeking God's direction for my life. God had called me to be a missionary in the South Pacific. Right now, I am in the process of seeing a 2-year prayer for vision be fulfilled. Words cannot describe the peace and joy that comes in knowing that the adventure that I am about to embark upon is not of my own design or manipulation. I never would have imagined that the vision I had been praying for would be mission work. And while I am so thankful and humbled to watch and see the Lord's hand at work, I realize that this is not the end: I have not "arrived," as they say. Yes, I know what step I am to take next, but I cannot see any farther down the path. We are called to wait for the Lord's leading, to follow when He calls, to travel by faith, and to worship along the way. It is in the journey, not the destination, in the waiting, not the pursuit, in the calling out and crying for vision, not in receiving the revelation itself that we build our faith and come to a deeper intimacy with our Creator. I encourage each of you to lay your dreams, desires, talents, and future before the Lord and boldly ask Him to reveal to you His vision for your life. He can be trusted.

—Age 24

God calls us to worship despite silence and fruitlessness—to be joyful in Him regardless of our circumstances. God moves most powerfully when we surrender our plans and desires to His will and control.

Remember that God's promises are bigger than sheltering us from emotions that make up life. He promises to love us, be with us, and guide us through all things. Don't fear the full range of emotions that are a part of life and don't let fear keep you from accepting the adventure that is the path God has laid before you. The way God leads may seem risky, but it's worth the risk!

Your Career Can Be a Ministry

I have found that you can minister to people in any career. I am a pediatric nurse and pray for God's light to shine through me each day. There are plenty of days when my duties are far from glamorous, although each child deserves the same loving care that Christ showed us. Whether a student, businesswoman, teacher, or nurse, your career can be a ministry if you desire it to be.

—Age 25

The "real world" can be a huge shock, but there are many joys that come with it. God will place many people in your life who do not share the same beliefs or value systems, but don't lose heart! This is your mission field!

Rejoice

Rejoice in what God has brought to you. When the dailiness of the work is at its very bleakest moment for you, look around. Your Father is at work.

—Age 27

Things are not going to work out exactly as you think. You can't control everything, make all the decisions, and call all the shots. Trust God! Contentment comes in knowing this. God knows what is best. Relax and hand it all over to Him. You will be so much happier! And if the vision is indeed from Him, He will orchestrate and fulfill it in His time and in His way.

How important to know that we are just where He wants us when tough times come—and they will. Know for a fact that with God you are never alone!

Dealing with Loneliness

Every person at one time or another has been lonely. This is a fact of life and can sometimes become extremely exaggerated in the real world, especially in the transitional stage after college. No one enjoys the feeling of isolation which can take place even in the most crowded room or crowded city. A 23-year-old speaks of her feelings while living in a huge city with lots of people, and yet sensing her aloneness.

> Having gone to a small, secluded college that prides itself, and rightfully so, on the incredible sense of community and fierce loyalty that it fosters in its students, the hardest part about graduating for me was simply the loneliness I felt from not being at this place that I loved so much. Suddenly, I lacked the sense of community, the intimacy, that I had thrived on for four years. I had moved to New York—a wonderful

city—but so completely different from the green, idyllic haven from which I had just departed that it only made the transition more poignant. I had friends who lived only a matter of blocks away, but somehow we now had different careers, different schedules, different lives. Many of my closest friends, people I had lived with at school and seen every day, were also in the city, but seeing them only once or twice a week made me feel as if our tight-knit friendships were crumbling. It was as if, having left school, I had lost a family. The good thing about this feeling, however, is that it does pass. As time goes on, you realize that your friends are still your friends, even if you don't see them every day, and that your new life can in time be one you love as much as your old. At least this is what I found. It can be a lonely transition, but it's not a crisis.

God did not intend for man to live a life of loneliness and it is His will that we use this feeling as a springboard to reach out of ourselves and to reach out to others.

> "And let us consider how we may spur one another on toward love and good deeds. Let us not give up meeting together, as some are in the habit of doing, but let us encourage one another—and all the more as you see the Day approaching."
> —Hebrews 10:24–25

A person's deepest needs are to love, be loved, and be held in high esteem by at least one other person. Loneliness is the feeling that comes when these needs are not being met. Jesus can meet all three of these needs. Through an intimate relationship with Him, loneliness can be crushed and solitude can be enjoyed—even treasured.

I wish I had known the joy of solitude earlier. In high school and college I think a lot of people equate their acceptance with the number of friends they have, and I know I did the same. It wasn't that I minded being alone, I just felt that I would be missing out if I weren't constantly doing something with my friends. I was very blessed to have such a close group of Christian girlfriends in high school as well as college and I never was forced to deal with being alone. Of course, everyone deals with loneliness even when surrounded by friends and family, but I never knew what it was to be alone and what kind of gifts God had in store for me. After college, I moved back home, panicked about who was going to live with me, and I was relieved to find two wonderful roommates. I just couldn't bear the thought of living alone and I don't know what made me think that was so terrible. I guess I thought "alone" equals lonely. Or worse, living alone means no one wants to live with you. After two years and many roommates, I made the decision to live on my own. Roommates are wonderful (if you have good ones, they can be wonderful accountability partners), but the time alone is such a different experience. My initial decision was made because I thought this "hardship" would make me a better person, more responsible. I guess it has, but it has offered me so much more. My relationship with God is more complete than it has been in such a long time. I had no idea my soul was starving for attention. The gift of singleness might be one of the best kept secrets. I wish I had known earlier that life alone could be so heavenly.

—Age 24

The introspection that loneliness brings can bring about many negative emotions. One such could be self-pity. This can lead to the thought that no one really cares about you. A 24-year-old woman was determined not to let self-pity grip her life as her new husband was called to Iraq. After receiving news of his absolute departure date, reality began to set in. She recalls, "I felt what I was sure hundreds of thousands of spouses across time experienced when their loved ones left for war. I imagined what WWI, WWII, Vietnam, and Desert Storm families went through and felt connected to a larger picture, one painted by generations of trials, courage, and pain when fathers, mothers, siblings, and children were sent to fight by the government." Although she considered herself to be strong and able to handle difficult situations, the night before his departure left her weak. Would he survive the war? Would this be their last goodbye? "They called my husband's unit and within five minutes he was gone. I stood alone, all at once both married and single. I was married to a man I loved deeply, and yet had to live as though I were single, taking care of the house, plans, and finances entirely by myself for the first time since our marriage began. In the end, it wasn't the bank account that became frustrating, but the times when I couldn't find something in the garage or needed to change a light bulb in our vaulted ceiling and couldn't reach it. The little things made me feel much lonelier than anything else. I really missed my partner."

In the following weeks, this young woman and many others banded together for support and friendship. Countless friends and strangers as well came forward to offer assistance and encouragement. Numerous emotions engulfed her heart—anxiety that a war would begin, fear that her husband would be killed or injured, sadness for the Americans, Iraqis, British, and others who had lost their lives in the battles. As the fighting ended she stated, "I became overwhelmingly lonely as it was the only emotion left standing after the others subsided." Prayer became her constant friend as she continued to pray for the safety of all while remaining realistic of the fact that her husband could potentially never return home.

"I learned to lay in quiet with God, not knowing how to ask what my heart felt, not knowing how to articulate my deepest fears and hopes. God answered me in my quiet and lonely space. My husband has not yet returned and I do not know the outcome of our situation yet, but I know there is peace in the depths of pain and I know there will be peace regardless of where this journey takes us."

Withdrawal can be another way of dealing with loneliness—removing yourself from others to avoid emotional pain. Sometimes it seems easier to just not deal with reality—to escape, go under. This is not the case for this 22-year-old woman after learning that she had been diagnosed with desmoid sarcoma for the third time in three years. She writes, "I can do all things through Christ who strengthens me.' I know that everyone has obstacles to overcome in life, but it hardly seemed fair when I was diagnosed with cancer for the third time. When I am overwhelmed, scared, lonely, or anxious, I focus on the fact that with God, my family, and my friends, I am going to fight this disease for as long as it persists and I will be a stronger person for it."

Rather than become frozen in fear, this young woman set goals for herself, and though many goals have become beyond her reach, she says, "Just yesterday I was diagnosed for my third time. This obstacle has kept me from reaching some of my goals, but it has allowed me to rethink what really matters in life and set new goals—goals that include using my experience to help others in similar situations. My newly-found cancer has not delayed my progress. In fact, it has only helped to motivate me to accomplish the goals that I have set. I do not feel sorry for myself or expect pity from others. In some ways my cancer has been a blessing. It has taught me so many important lessons that I will take with me for the rest of my life. It has brought me closer to my family and to God and has made me realize my passion for helping others. I have learned to appreciate the smaller things in life and take nothing for granted. I am thankful that I have opportunities to help others like others have helped me."

Loneliness can cause sarcasm. It becomes self-satisfying to speak unkindly about others who seem to have it all together. This can cause a fear which will make you not even desire to reach out, a feeling of uselessness, of having nothing to offer others. All of these feelings of loneliness can only add to feelings of frustration and helplessness.

How can I break the habit of loneliness? Be honest with yourself, others, and most importantly, God.

"Cast all your anxiety on him because he cares for you."
—1 Peter 5:7

"Therefore each of you must put off falsehood and speak truthfully to his neighbor."
—Ephesians 4:25

As we face the fact that we are lonely, we can ask others for help and, most of all, ask God to help us. This does not make a person weak.

The year after I graduated college was probably one of the worst years of my life this far. I just felt so awkward, far more awkward than I had ever felt at thirteen. I was depressed about everything. I felt like all I did was go to work, come home, eat, sleep, and start it all over again. And I didn't see any light at the end of the tunnel, either. My outlook on the future was so bleak. I thought, "I worked my entire life to get here. Why?" I had wonderful friends, but I was still lonely. I didn't see how I was ever going to meet new people, in particular available guys. I was just so overwhelmed by all the responsibilities that a grownup life included. I had looked forward to this stage of life for as long as I could remember. It was so disappointing.

—Age 23

Realize that God wants you to have friends. The second most important thing that I can do in life is to love my neighbor as myself. God commands it and Jesus is our example for relationships. He stayed in close communion with God and also had close friends on earth. We will never be truly lonely if we have a close walk with Jesus Christ, as a 23-year-old testifies in facing the loneliness of the real world.

> Also, one thing that I think helped was a Bible my mom gave me, one of those where you read certain passages on certain days, and if you keep up, you'll have read the entire Bible in a year. I found it really beneficial because it gave me a regimented way to spend more time with God. Not only did I start reading more of the Bible each day than I had previously been in the habit of doing, but it reminded me that the Christian community is a community that I have no matter where I am and that communion with God can be as tangible as the friendships I have from school. I think a certain part of me will always miss my college days, but I no longer feel lonely like I initially did. Now I am just thankful for the experiences and memories I have, knowing that the future holds many more.

Jesus was never lonely because God was always with Him.

> "Surely I am with you always, to the very end of the age."

—Matthew 28:20

In a practical way, I can commune with God daily by prayer and Bible study. If God's Holy Spirit lives within you, you will never be alone, even if there is no one around you in a physical way.

So, what if you choose to move to a new city or live alone? Listen to the following perspectives.

My best advice for women leaving college and entering the workforce is to move someplace new, on your own if possible. It is too easy to head back home or to live and work in a city where you are surrounded by family or friends. If it is feasible, move to a new city where you know no one. You'll be forced to make all new friends, negotiate your way around a new city, and spend lots of time by yourself with only your thoughts for company. There is no better way to find out just how strong and resourceful you really are. You can always move back to the comfort of family and friends, but it will be with a greater understanding of who you are and what you are capable of accomplishing on your own.

—Age 27

Living alone gave me a chance to see myself for who I really am. I grew into the person I am today partly because of my choice to live alone. After living alone, for the first time in my life, I was not scared to be alone. Sure, I was lonely for awhile and the first few months were not always the best. But now, I cherish time alone (and, of course, I have a lot less of it now that I am married!). God used loneliness to teach me to truly be myself and allow Him to mold and use me in ways I could never have imagined. I learned things about myself that I may have never discovered if He didn't allow me to learn to be alone.

—Age 26

Like most college girls, I spent those four college years in cramped, messy, claustrophobic, fun living situations. It started in the dorm, ended in the sorority house, and sandwiched between were two years in a nasty 8-bedroom house with 3 bathrooms. Needless to say, by graduation, I was in dire need of space. A friend and I moved into an apartment but even that wasn't enough. A grueling job search that caused unexpected frustration, struggling with wanting to be married but knowing it was too early, and the tight living quarters contributed to my snappy demeanor—I was a terrible roommate. If you feel you may have this disposition, consider living alone for awhile. It was the best thing I could have ever done for myself, my relationships, and my job.

—Age 28

The real world invites you to live on your own. Pay your own bills to become, in a word, independent. Don't allow this independence to make you self-centered, seeing everything from your own needs and perspectives. If we really want to get out of loneliness, we must forget about ourselves and reach out to others in a giving way. This will cost involvement, but it is worth it all.

September 11, 2001, changed the course of our nation and the way of life for so many. A 24-year-old woman became a part of the drama that morning as she worked in the building directly next to the World Trade towers. "I had moved to New York two months prior to begin my new job after college. It was the first time I had ever lived for an extended period of time outside my home state, so, needless to say, I had a lot of adjusting to do. Never was I prepared for the events that would occur that beautiful Tuesday morning."

On that particular morning she had gone into work early to finish up a presentation that her group head was going to make.

Carrying the fifty copies for the presentation, she heard a booming noise and felt her building shake. Thinking something had exploded downstairs, she prayed for protection and continued to her group head's office. Through his window she saw the flames, breaking glass, and debris flying through the air. After calling her mother to let her know she was safe, she joined a group of colleagues in an office that looked out at the towers. They watched in horror as the building burned. Being on the 42nd floor made the fire feel even closer. "I didn't like watching but I didn't want to be alone. I saw someone jump and felt my eyes well up with tears. A feeling of sickness overcame me. I couldn't get his face and billowing jacket and outstretched arms out of my mind. I prayed for the man who jumped and the other people in the tower. I continued to pray for protection. I couldn't watch anymore, so I looked away at the second tower. It was then that I saw an airplane coming and let out a scream and practically jumped on the ground as, from my vantage point, it looked like the plane was coming for us. I saw the plane crash into the second tower just before I ducked."

Chaos broke out in her office as colleagues bumped into each other, coffee cups flying. The young woman grabbed a coworker and begged him not to leave her as they started running down the 42 flights of stairs. As more people began to evacuate, their running slowed or even halted. "At times I began to panic and could feel my legs locking. I kept praying that I could get one leg in front of the other. I looked at all the people around me and wondered how many knew Jesus. I prayed the entire way down and kept repeating the following verse: 'For God did not give us a spirit of timidity, but a spirit of power, of love and of self-discipline' (2 Timothy 1:7)."

It took 45 minutes to get out of the building. The duo ran toward the river, resting briefly on a park bench to catch their breath. The burning towers transfixed hundreds. "I had a feeling something horrible was about to happen. We ran up the West

Side Highway. I shared my faith with my friend as to how much we needed Jesus Christ. I felt many people were in prayer around me. I didn't know how to begin to bring the unsaved to Jesus amongst strangers running for their lives. This is something I will never forget, and I pray God will use me to bring others to Him."

As this young woman and her friend arrived at her apartment, the first tower fell. "The rest of the day was suspended in time for me. It's hard to put into words how isolated I felt. I was carried by the continuous stream of calls and prayers that I received. Still, at the end of the day, I was alone and scared and felt removed from the world I once knew. I stayed in constant conversation with God that night, as I couldn't sleep. I reached out for Him and He provided me with comfort. I was one of the fortunate ones. 'In repentance and rest is your salvation, in quietness and trust is your strength' (Isaiah 30:15)."

In times you are alone, think about the lonely people everywhere and decide that you are going to be sensitive to them and reach out to them. Most importantly, tell them about Jesus.

> Make your peace with family, friends, and the Lord while you're still young and healthy. I moved to New York City 10 days before September 11, 2001—I watched the second tower fall from the roof of my apartment building. Those people got up and went to work—they never thought they wouldn't come home that day. That day made an impression on me, as it did for most Americans. I never hang up the phone with the people I love without saying, "I love you." Even though they know, I want them to hear it from me."
>
> —Age 24

Will I view my life as a twentysomething as a crisis or opportunity? Life is short even at its longest.

seventeen

Quarter-Life
Crisis Declared Over

"*I* am young in years,
   and you are old;
that is why I was fearful,
   not daring to tell you what I know.
I thought, 'Age should speak;
   advanced years should teach wisdom.'
But it is the spirit in a man,
   the breath of the Almighty, that gives him
   understanding.
It is not only the old who are wise,
   not only the aged who understand what is right."
                                        —Job 32:6–9

Many believe that success depends only upon education, talent, or
brilliance. For others, it's getting the breaks, being in the right place

at the right time, or pulling the right strings. It never hurts to know the right people—to look good and be seen. Our natural tendency is to be overly impressed with the external. How important to look for and detect the deeper things such as character and heart! As we view life from the heart, and more specifically, the heart of God, it becomes quite evident that age has very little to do with how much a person achieves, and absolutely nothing to do with commitment.

There is a difference between natural sight and supernatural vision. When we look at life through the eyes of God, we perceive events and circumstances from an eternal perspective. In every circumstance of life, God's thoughts are higher and more profound than our way of thinking and perceiving. By lining our thoughts up with God's, there is hope when all may appear hopeless, frustrating, disorganized, or chaotic.

The real world can be a scary place—a place in which to get lost. Hang tough! Face it when you feel like it and when you'd rather not. Deal with it when you're up and when you're down. Charge ahead when it comes naturally and when it's not so easy. Do not give up! Be persistent and determined.

Remain Steadfast

Stand out—remain steadfast! Keep praying. Remain faithful in your quiet times and get involved spiritually where you are planted. Seek out accountability. Don't get lost in this "real world." College was a place where others generally knew what you stood for. In the real world, for me, it's harder to make a stand without being utterly bold, direct, and open about who you are. I don't really socialize with many of my coworkers outside of work, so in the workplace I could ostensibly create whatever identity I want to have.

—Age 24

There is pressure in the real world to be assertive and professional. If you are a young, effervescent, friendly, and eager woman, your intelligence or assertiveness may be discounted. There's a pressure to be hard—to appear stronger. Remember, real strength comes from God through the power of the Holy Spirit. How important to clothe yourself with this power through morning prayer! In this way you will be able to rise above the little worldly deceits that so easily entangle us, and not only to work hard and excel in the office, but also to be open to the needs of others. The world is a lonely place with many hurting hearts. Christians carry the cure! So remain steadfast in your own heart and be fishers of men wherever God places you in the world.

There is not one set way to fullness of life. There is not one solution or one framework that defines the perfect, most satisfying way. We are all on different journeys in this world, moving at different speeds and going in different directions. I emphasize the word journey because we will not arrive at our destination in this lifetime. Our hearts will continue to long for more until we go home to heaven.

The Gifts of Instability

We are all different. The sooner we accept this truth, the sooner we can stop vainly trying to make ourselves match someone else and open ourselves to freely receive the unique gifts that God longs to give us now.

When life made sense to me and went according to the pace I set, my identity became rooted in my circumstances. As my circumstances changed quickly, I painfully realized that I wasn't sure of who I was and what God's plans for me were. Nevertheless, it was only by moving to a place of instability that my eyes were opened to this. God reminded me that I must trust my identity solely in Christ to find freedom from others' expectations of what I should be doing. When we find ourselves in places that seem dark and doubtful, defined by the unknown, that's when we can truly know "God-with-us," the God who "never leaves us forsakes us." And only then have we found peace. We are able to understand that life need not be predictable to be enjoyable and that only by lifting our hands with open palms to whatever God may have for us, may we begin to taste the full life that Jesus came to give us to enjoy right now, wherever we may be.

—Age 23

Looking for Your Passion

I felt overwhelmed as I tried to plan the next step after graduating from college. I was unable to find my career path and passion. I searched monster.com and asked everybody about their jobs. I asked how they found out they should be in their field, and what prepared them for the work involved. I still came up short and continued to question why I had no particular career path and passion to pursue. I knew I would stumble on something, whether great or small, and would be able to identify and pursue it when the time was right.

My fiancé saw that my need to find a career path was disturbing my enjoyment of life. He told me I was wonderful, loved, and needed only to relax, take a deep breath, and enjoy life. Through his encouragement, I was able to say, "Life is beautiful, fragile, and short. I have so many wonderful people around me who love and support me. I should be thankful, enjoying each new experience, never giving up— with a smile on my face and in my heart."

—Age 22

Praise God in all things and in all circumstances. This takes practice, as it is not familiar to our flesh. Pride is put aside in order to enter into praise and the tangible presence of God. The devil will not hang around for this. Worship, exalt, and acknowledge that God is worthy. In doing this we are saying that despite our circumstances, problems, hurts, and confusion, we are still counting on God our Father.

Praise Is Not Formal

When I talk about praise it is not something formal. Praise to me is singing a song, playing music, something like that. God is moved by our humbling ourselves to tell Him that we love Him. We are His children and nothing else pleases Him more. Praise breaks any hold that the enemy has on us and it threatens him. He will not stay around for that, and there is an immediate release for God's glory in our lives.

—Age 24

God honors our waiting on Him. He is always working things out for our good. His intentions are never meant to harm or hurt us. A lot of times people would like to blame God for their problems or troubles when often it is the consequence of our own sin. By being patient and waiting for His plan we can rise up on wings of eagles—walk and not grow faint—run and not be weary!

God's Unconditional Love

"For the wages of sin is death, but the gift of God is eternal life in Christ Jesus our Lord" (Romans 6:23). How many times have I heard this verse? How many times I repeated it from memory to others. It seems to be one of the most popular verses in Christian circles. However, I am still learning the depths of this promise. I accepted the gospel at a young age, but I never really have understood the depth of His love. Romans 6:23 is a promise to God's beloved, that He has forgiven you, that no matter what you do God sees you as His bride—pure and beautiful.

As a believer in Jesus Christ, there is nothing you will or can ever do or achieve to make God love you more than He already does right now. We tend to look to beauty, academics, wealth, fame, jobs, family, friends, love, etc. for our identity. There is nothing wrong with having any of these things as long as you know that none of those things will fulfill you. As a believer in Jesus Christ, our confidence is in this: "For God so loved the world that he gave his one and only Son, that whoever believes in him shall not perish but have eternal life" (John 3:16).

—Age 26

Accepting Jesus Christ as your personal Lord and Savior is the most important decision you'll ever make. When you do this or if you already are a believer, the next step is to study God's Word. Use the Bible as your instruction book for life. As far as your place in this world, start with the question: "What are my strengths?" When you answer this question about yourself, begin to look for opportunities to use your gifts to serve the Lord. And as college fades and the real world looms, look forward, not backward.

Moving On After College

When it was said and done, and pictures came off the wall, and clothes were taken out of dorm closets, the blanket of anxiety covered me. I looked around the room at these people who only four short years ago I did not know, and hadn't even heard of the towns they were from, but over time became some of my best friends. I was leaving them. It's okay to be sad, to be worried, to feel anxious, to feel scared. It's not okay, however, to live in the past. Part of the beauty of the life experience is that it's a journey, a walk; walking backwards will only make the journey that much more difficult and getting to the next interesting stop on the trip that much farther away.

—Age 24

Experience Life

Go out and experience life and your youth. We won't be this young forever! Spend time with your friends. Don't sweat the small stuff, which includes most everything! Whenever I complained of being tired, not wanting to do something, my friend always chided, "You can catch up on your sleep when you die!"

—Age 26

While compiling advice for this book, I was asked to speak about twentysomethings in the real world to a group of young women at a large church. I shared openly of plans and events in my own life. Afterwards I received this letter from a 23-year-old who attended the meeting. She had been discouraged until that evening.

Quarter-Life Crisis Over

Early this year, I got to hear you speak. I could not hold back the tears. I'm not really sure what caused the floodgates to open. But your plans sounded so similar to mine: Get married after college, have four kids, etc. Yet you had never gotten married. And you are one of the most amazing women I've ever met! I began to realize that God's plans may be different, but they are also the best for us. You also made me see how ridiculous this quarter-life crisis thing really is. When you talked about drawing closer to God during this time in our lives, I realized that had been my problem. In all the other difficult times in my life, I had drawn closer to God. Freshman year of college was a prime example. However, for some inexplicable reason, once I hit the real world I did not. If anything, I pulled away from Him. Then you quoted the one verse that God has used more than once in my life to speak to me: "'For I know the plans I have for you,' declares the LORD, 'plans to prosper you and not to harm you, plans to give you hope and a future'" (Jeremiah 29:11). Afterward, I officially declared my quarter-life crisis over! I joined the church the next weekend. I had peace about everything, and most importantly, contentment. That doesn't mean that everything in my life is perfect, but I feel whole again and happy.

—Age 23

"Teach us to number our days aright, that we may gain a heart of wisdom."

—Psalm 90:12

Contributors to This Book

Jenna Poole Abel—Washington and Lee University, Vanderbilt Divinity
   School
Jennifer Abernathy—Louisiana State University
Kate Adams—University of Mississippi
Katherine Alford—University of Virginia
Lucy Anderson—University of Alabama
Amy Thompson Appleby—Auburn University
Sally Moody Baker—Washington and Lee University, University of
   Alabama
Katie Baldwin—Washington and Lee University, The Courtauld
   Institute of Art-University of London
Betsy Thomas Barlow—Auburn University, University of Montevallo
Ashley Kensinger Batcheller—Washington and Lee University
Catherine McIntosh Bentley—Auburn University
Margaret Cooper Biggs—Hollins University
Wellon Lee Bridgers—Auburn University, Wake Forest University
Leslie Denton Brooks—University of Mississippi, University of
   Alabama at Birmingham
Jennifer Wilson Buckley—University of Alabama at Birmingham
Callie Campbell—Washington and Lee University, University of South
   Carolina School of Law
Clare Canzoneri—Indiana University
Caitie Cataldo—Duke University
Mary Margaret Chambliss—Presbyterian College, Rocky Mountain
   School of Photography
Jennie Clay—University of Texas-Austin
J. Jaye Northcut Cole—Samford University, New Orleans Baptist
   Theological Seminary
Jill Suitts Coleman—Auburn University
Christen Colvert—Auburn University
Kate Stutts Comini—University of Mississippi, Samford University
Melissa Craig—Samford University, University of Alabama at
   Birmingham
Kessley Carraway Crowe—University of Mississippi
Hallet Davis—Washington and Lee University
Kate deFuniak—University of Mississippi
Jeanne Upchurch de Lauréal—Washington and Lee University,
   University of North Carolina at Charlotte

Kristen Denson—Hollins University
Kami Dipoma—Weber State Univesity
Kathryn Millirons Dumas—Southern Methodist University
Berdine Edgar—Washington and Lee University, Medical University of
    South Carolina
Crandall Sproul Edwards—Auburn University
Allen Clare Elkins—Washington and Lee University
Emily Putnam Fulton—Auburn University
Katie St. Claire Garrett—Furman University
Kathleen Ann Gibson—Washington and Lee University
Emily deFuniak Gregory—University of Mississippi
Holly Hall—Auburn University, University of Alabama at Birmingham
Kappi Hamilton—Auburn University
Kate Wood Hamilton—University of Alabama
Anne Frost Hawker—Spring Hill College, University of South Alabama
Mary Margaret Hiller—Auburn University
Rebecca Hiller—Auburn University, University of Southern California
Whitney Holladay—Auburn University
Karen Schliesser Holley—Auburn University
Shannon Upchurch Holt—Washington and Lee University, Vanderbilt
    School of Law
Libby Kendall House—Auburn University
Lisa Bunting Howard—Wheaton College-Massachusetts, University of
    Alabama School of Social Work
Amy Hudson—Covenant College
Jessica Hudson—Covenant College, University of Kentucky
Sara J. Hume—University of Virginia
Katie McDowell Issak—Auburn University
Katherine Jackson—Wheaton College-Illinois, Bryn Mawr Medical
    School
Olivia Erickson Jackson—Auburn University, Chongqing University
    (China)
Rebecca James—Auburn University, University of California-Los Angeles
Jennifer Jeffords—Samford University
Leah Johnson—University of Alabama at Birmingham
Jennifer Lell Jones—Spring Hill College, Samford University
Lindy Simpson Jones—Auburn University, David Lipscomb University
Rachael McIntosh Jordan—Auburn University
Kate Kelley—Auburn University
Neillie Kirk—University of Alabama
Liza Tucker Koch—Washington and Lee University
Karen Old Lathram—Auburn University, University of Alabama

Elizabeth Dreher Lawrence—Auburn University, Parsons School of
     Design, Cumberland School of Law
Sara Louise Joy Lawson—Azusa Pacific University (California), George
     Fox University, Western Seminary (Portland, Oregon)
Pamela DeBardeleben Leonard—Auburn University
Catherine Caldwell Lipsey—Washington and Lee University, Gordon
     Conwell Seminary
Lucy McDonald—Emory University
Maggie McDonald—Rhodes College, Washington University-St. Louis
Ellen Magnus—Auburn University
Caroline Dumas Malatesta—Washington and Lee University
Mary Anna Hemphill Malone—Auburn University
Molly Martin—Vanderbilt University
Colin McRae Mitchell—University of Virginia
Dottie Mitchell—The School of the Art Institute of Chicago
Brooke Moor—University of Alabama
Emily Moore—Texas A&M University
Bethany Moore—Oral Roberts University
Alex Morris—Dartmouth College
Claire Bondurant Myers—Auburn University
Mindi Myser—The Ohio State University
Elizabeth Nacozy—Washington and Lee University, Vanderbilt University
Margaret Naftel—Vanderbilt University
Leslie Old—Auburn University
Lesley Ann Howell Owen—Samford University
Kam Waitzman Patton—University of Alabama
Amy Perez—Auburn University
Anna Veren Perry—Auburn University
Bragan Dreher Petrey—Vanderbilt University
Bradford Greene Phelan—Auburn University
Carrie Pittman—Southern Methodist University
Burgin Powell—University of Alabama
Mary Britt Adams Redden—Vanderbilt University
Caroline Cater Reynolds—Rhodes College
Elizabeth Alford Rice—Washington and Lee University
Leah Thomas Rice—Auburn University
Laura Roberts—University of Alabama
Cindy L. Rodriguez—Harvard University
Melanie Rogers—Auburn University, Reformed Theological Seminary
Andrea Rose—Urban Bible Training Center
Courtney Rosenthal—Washington and Lee University
Elizabeth Sandner—University of Mississippi

Deborah Sands—Florida Southern College
Elizabeth Saxton—Washington and Lee University, University of
    Tennessee School of Law
Crystal Simpson—Washington and Lee University
Tyler Sims—University of Alabama
Leigh Norris Smith—Auburn University, University of Alabama at
    Birmingham
Sarah Clements Smyth—Judson College
Meeghan Callahan Sowinski—Furman University, University of South
    Carolina
Camille Spratling—Birmingham Southern College
Lauren Watkins Stahl—Vanderbilt University
Allison Duncan Stallcup—Auburn University
Laura Glenn Steele—University of Mississippi
Meredith Stinson—University of Alabama
Erica Suares—Auburn University
Holly DuBrowa Sutherland—Shepherd College (Shepherdstown, West
    Virginia), Lindsey Wilson College (Columbia, Kentucky)
Candice Patton Tompkins—University of Missouri
Sarah Torsch—Auburn University, Birmingham Theological Seminary
Forrest Walker Turner—University of Alabama
Eleanor Twiford—University of Mississippi
Kit Upchurch—Presbyterian College, Wheaton College-Illinois
Caroline Voitier—Auburn University
Neeva Walker—Chico State University, Chatham College
Rushton Mellen Waltchack—Auburn University
Charlotte Gage Walton—University of Mississippi
Clayton Kearse Walton—Converse College
Brooks Chappelle Wellmon—Davidson College
Mallie Mitchell Whatley—University of Virginia, Fashion Institute of
    Technology-New York City
Margaret Saunders Whittenburg—University of Alabama
Alison Wiggers—Mississippi State University
Hollie Wohlwend—Carson Newman College, Beeson Divinity School
Martha Jane Wood Wolters—University of Mississippi, Covenant
    Theological Seminary
Leslie Ann Sheppard Wood—Furman University
Marne Mink Wood—University of Alabama
Elizabeth Hays Wood—University of Mississippi
Ruth Hill Yeilding—Washington and Lee University, University of
    Alabama School of Medicine
Anne Yoder—Auburn University